THE BIGGEST
LIE

AND
THE GREATEST TRUTH

BRIAN H BUTLER

Chart comparing Religion and Theology

RELIGION	THEOLOGY
GOD GOD'S WORD The Holy Bible	**GOD** GOD'S WORD The Holy Bible
FILTER 1 The Human Mind The carnal mind is enmity against God, for it is not subject to the law of God, neither indeed can be Romans 8:7	THE PURPOSE OF LIFE is to learn about God from the study of His Word & to strive to be like Him. Ask for, and receive it! GOD'S HOLY SPIRIT FLOWS INTO YOUR MIND The 'Light' comes on. New Understanding floods your mind & heart.
FILTER 2 Truth mixed with error Partial truths False Doctrines - Idolatry Human ideas & reasonings	**NO FILTERS** PURE TRUTH DIRECT FROM GOD TO YOU
FILTER 3 Church organisations Priests, Ministers Desire to control followers	**YOU** YOUR MIND Your Human Spirit Enlightened by the flow of God's Holy Spirit, filled with the truth The eyes of your understanding being enlightened; that you may know what is the hope of His calling, and what the Riches of the Glory of His inheritance in the saints. And what is the exceeding greatness of His Power to us-ward who believe, according to the working of His Mighty Power. Ephesians 1:18-19
YOU YOUR MIND Your Human Spirit Deceived into believing truth mixed with error Having the understanding darkened being alienated from the life of God through the ignorance that is in them, because of the blindness of their heart Ephesians 4:18	

©Copyright 2017 Brian H. Butler

TABLE OF CONTENTS

CHAPTER 4

CHAPTER 5

CHAPTER 6

CHAPTER 7

THE MYSTERY REVEALED -   THE GREATEST TRUTH

Acknowledgement & Dedication

In all my seventy-eight years I had often been exhorted to study the Bible, but I had *never* been taught *how* properly to study.

Dr. Ernest L. Martin, my colleague and mentor, showed me HOW to study. The first essential tool is always to begin by asking for God's help for inspiration and understanding. The wonderful Bible study 'tools' I have learned from Dr. Martin and his tapes, also form the basis of this book, 'The Biggest Lie'.

Sadly Dr. Martin died in January 2002.

A personal note from the author:

"I have absolutely no doubt in my mind that in this age, Dr. Martin was a (if not the) most remarkable teacher filled with the Holy Spirit, and that his insights and research were guided directly by God. I have found his work more inspiring than the work of any other man in my now eighty-two years. But please be very clear, in no way am I 'following a man', but merely using his tools. I am following Christ's Word, studying the Bible for myself, with God's help".

Dr. Martin hoped that many would 'do him out of a job' by learning with the aid of Christ and the Holy Spirit so that we will not even have to learn from him. (Or from me! Ed.) Dr. Martin says we have never really needed him, and that may be true, but I feel that God has used him to help me grow in grace and knowledge by leaps and bounds using the 'tools of the trade' he recommended; compared to sixty years of a lifetime of personal study in my own strength.

I truly hope that the same may become true for those who read this book.

ACKNOWLEDGEMENT & DEDICATION

Preface - How this book came to be written

As a child, my parents used to take me to church. When I was about twelve, I was asked to give the reading which happened to be 1 Corinthians 13, known as the 'Love' chapter. I memorised it, and somehow, its content and the occasion remained with me. Although attending for many years, my whole experience could be summed up by saying, I never really understood anything. The odd parable, or the story of Jonah, but otherwise, nothing.

Once I left home at eighteen when I was called up to do my National Service in the R.A.F., I did not attend any services at all. At twenty-two, I once went to a local church, but was so unimpressed, I never went again. I had always believed in God, and thought of Him as Creator, but I really was not interested at all in any religion. Frankly, even then, I thought, like so many do, that religious activities seemed to be at the root of many of the world's problems and wars.

Then I got the 'flu. Confined to bed, I started to browse some old copies of the Reader's Digest. Some advertisements took my eye. One said in bold lettering, 'Does God Exist?'. Another offered 'Proof of the Bible'. There was no mention of a church, just the offer of some leaflets. I sent off for them.

I was taken by the style of the pamphlets, and that the writer clearly believed that the Bible was actually, really, the Word of God. Something went on in my mind, and I was very keen to learn more.

After a year or so of studying the written material and the Bible, I came to realise that there was an organisation behind it all, a church. I wrote off to them, and to cut a long story short, when I was twenty-five, I was invited to attend.

My first experience in the dingy, dusty hall was not enjoyable at all. The congregation seemed to be a motley group of somewhat miserable people. Anyway, I was not looking for a cosy social club. I was looking for more inspiration to read and study the Bible, and to come to a better understand what this word 'Christian' was all about, so I stuck with it.

Most of the ministers were a sombre lot, and the sermons were long and not very interesting. An exception was a Dr. Ernest L. Martin, who seemed very different from all the others. His approach to the Bible, his historical and chronological knowledge, and the way he told us to read the Scriptures carefully, impressed and inspired me to greater efforts.

At twenty-nine, in 1964, I applied to go to the college which was run by the church, and was accepted for the four year, full time course, to major in Theology and obtain a Bachelor of Arts degree.

During my four years in college, I was privileged to take several courses with Dr. Ernest L. Martin, the Dean of the Faculty. His lectures were always riveting, and the most enjoyable as he made the history, geography, and the chronology of the Bible 'come alive' as I had never experienced in my life before.

After graduation in 1968, I was offered the opportunity to work for the College, and I gladly accepted a position in the data processing department, which was to stand me in good stead as time went on.

I also spent time with Dr. Martin between 1971-1974 after I was appointed a member of the Faculty of Ambassador College, Bricket Wood, U.K.

In 1974, Dr. Martin was the head of the department of Theology at the headquarters of the church in Pasadena, California. His personal studies over several years, independent of the church hierarchy, led him to realise that many of the doctrines taught by the church did not stack up against what the Bible clearly said. In fact many flatly contradicted what the Bible said.

Dr. Martin attempted on many occasions to bring to the notice of the church doctrinal committee for their consideration, anomalies and deviations from what the Bible plainly showed. His attempts were always met with hostility and rebuttal. As a result of these unresolved differences over most important matters. So after forty years of service with the church as a high ranking minister, Dr. Martin saw not other recourse but to resign his position as Head of Theology. His letter of resignation may be viewed at:

https://hwarmstrong.com/history/history-earnest-martin-resignation.htm

In 1975, my work with that church came to an end. Two years previously, in 1973, I had met and spent time with an American Chiropractor, Dr. John Blossom, who introduces me to a new concept in chiropractic, known as Applied Kinesiology (A.K.) developed by Dr. George Goodheart.

For the next twenty-five years I pioneered A.K. in Britain and Europe, ran a clinic of natural health care, and taught thousands the A.K. principles of self-help health care.

In 2000, I retired after those years working in natural health care, helping the sick to work on their health and well-being, I once again turned to the study of Theology. The word Theology comes from two Greek words, Theo meaning God, and Logos meaning Word, hence Theology is the study of God's Word, the Holy Bible.

More recently, in 2013 I began an intense and in-depth study of over two hundred tapes recorded, and articles written by Dr. Martin on the fruits of his many years of Biblical research. These tapes were kindly sent to me by Ken Nagele, custodian and designer of the www.ernestlmartin.com website.

Working with Dr. Martin's material for 40-50 hours a week, using the essential 'keys' to understanding the Bible that he suggested the earnest Bible student employed, I learned more in those three years than I had in over sixty years of my own personal previous study of the Holy Bible in my own strength. Since 2013 I have written well over a thousand pages of notes on Dr. Martin's Biblical doctrinal research. In my opinion this article contains the most important details of the fundamental basis of Christianity.

I became so excited at what I was learning about HOW to study the Bible with God's help, rather than accepting what any church or minister told me about it, or trying to study in my own strength. I wanted to share my new knowledge and approach with others. So I wrote 'Why ARE We Here?' a 438 page book which gave proof of the Authority and accuracy of the Bible, and the essential 'Keys' to a proper approach to the study of the Scriptures. and is available in e-book form completely free from www.ernestworkman.com Or retail as an ebook or printed paperback from Amazon.com

In 2017, I embarked on this current volume which contains the evidence of the deception of 'Churchianity, and the 'Theory of Evolution', and more importantly, gives the 'Keys' on HOW to study, and grow in Grace and Knowledge, and a glimpse of the glorious future we have as Children of God.

Introduction, Purpose & Goals

The purpose and goals of this book, 'The Biggest Lie' is to provide a resource to anyone whose 'eyes and ears' are being opened by our Father, the Almighty God.

God, by means of the flow of His Power, Holy Spirit will inspire their minds, to see the clear evidence of deception that Christ Jesus warned about in Revelation, the last Book of the Bible He wrote for our instruction.

*Revelation 12:9 And **the** great dragon was cast out, that old serpent, called **the** Devil, and Satan, which deceiveth **the** **whole world**: he was cast out into **the** earth, and his angels were cast out with him.*

When Christ says that Satan has deceived the whole world, He means just that.

That includes all organisations of human beings. The Governments, the Philosophers, Scientists, the Religions, are all involved in the greatest deception possible.

In the realm of religions for instance, there are over thirty thousand separate denominations of what is known as Christianity. Each one claims that their version of the truth, what they believe, teach and practice from their understanding of the Bible, is the correct one. They cannot all be right! There can only be one version of the Truth. The Holy Bible is that Truth.

The original manuscripts, inspired by Christ were the source of the Bible we have today, and they were perfect, exactly as He intended them to be.

However, all human translations contain errors, made either by translators, or by organisations which have altered the Bible to suit their own agendas.

The earnest student of the Bible need not be concerned too much about the aberrations, as it is perfectly possible, with God's help, to find a way past those errors, and be assured that what they are learning is indeed the Truth.

Repetition for Emphasis

This book, like the Bible, contains a lot of apparent repetition. This is intentional. Because God uses repetition in His Word for emphasis of important matters; I use repetition for emphasis in this book.

We are bombarded 24/7 by Satan's Anti-God repetitive propaganda through all forms of media. The television, radio, newspapers, and the internet, all give emphasis to anti-God information. Much of what we see and hear gets into our minds and hearts without our knowing it. Our minds are all influenced by this whether we realise it or not. This is one subtle way Satan deceives the whole world.

So in this book, many important and essential points are repeated in similar ways in an attempt, hopefully, to help the reader to cleanse their minds of this evil influence with 'the washing of water by the Word'.

CHAPTER 1

THE BIGGEST LIE – "YOU SHALL NOT DIE"

Is there a life after death?

It is estimated that over 94% of the seven billion people on this Earth believe that part of a human being lives on after death.

All the four religions which originated in the Indian sub-continent believe in Reincarnation. Hinduism, which is thought to be as old as humanity, grew out of a way of life, and was not formed by any individual. Jainism, Buddhism, Islam, Sikhism were all formed around the 6th century A.D.

Reincarnation

Billions of people on Earth claim that 'justification' or development towards 'enlightenment' comes after several lives lived out on this Earth. This claim is according to the teaching of those who believe in 'Reincarnation'. However, they either know nothing of Christianity, and dismiss or refute the fact that the Bible says justification comes by faith in Christ and His resurrection from the *dead*.

We absolutely do not have to go through various lives, either as humans, or as some think different creatures, gradually improving our spiritual nature in order to be justified by Christ! That would be a doctrine of 'works' to gain Salvation, and we know that just is not true.

This truth is that most only get one human life. The only exceptions will be those who will be resurrected to human life who were blinded by God, and never had a proper chance of understanding the truth, and will be resurrected later to be given that chance.

Romans 4:24 But for us also, to whom it shall be imputed, if we believe on him that raised up Jesus our Lord from the dead; 25 Who was delivered for our offences, and was raised again for our justification.

Many people in the limelight, actors, film stars, and others who have the public's attention are currently talking and writing about all types of 'spirit' experiences, including 'out of body experiences'. Some who think they have apparently come back from 'the dead' in a hospital tell of how wonderful their 'death experiences' were. But of course whatever they thought, they experienced in their consciousness while apparently 'dead'. They were either the product of their own minds, or actually 'spirit' induced, because according to the Bible they were NOT DEAD. Again:-

Ecclesiastes 9:10 Whatsoever thy hand findeth to do, do it with thy might; for there is no work, nor device, nor knowledge, nor wisdom, in the grave, whither thou goest.

Other notables are in our era write biographies about those who have had other types of 'spiritual' experiences, or contacts with 'spirits', or 'life after a '*death*' visions on the operating table' All of which adds to the tide of 'evidence' to those who choose to believe in the 'spirit' living on after death.

All these reports are total nonsense; they are coming from their own minds or other sources, the evil 'spirits' that throng the ether surrounding this world. In Christ's time, He spent a lot of time casting spirits out of people.

Luke 8:29 (For he had commanded the unclean spirit to come out of the man. For oftentimes it had caught him: and he was kept bound with chains and in fetters; and he brake the bands, and was driven of the devil into the wilderness.)

In Christ's lifetime, some had many 'spirits' possessing them as undoubtedly is the same today, often in the case of the criminally insane.

Mark 5:8 For he said unto him, Come out of the man, thou unclean spirit. 9 And he asked him, What is thy name? And he answered, saying, My name is Legion: for we are many.

We can have the protection of God daily when we pray to be delivered from the evil ones.

Greek philosophers around the 4ᵗʰ century B.C., who spread immoral practices, also promoted this teaching, and had an influence on those who embraced early Christianity.

Do you go to heaven when you die?
The majority of Christians believe that when you die, you go to heaven. Satan has been very successful in convincing almost everyone that death does not mean death, but means a continuation of consciousness, either in heaven, or Reincarnation, or by some other mechanism. Satan's other masterstroke is to get everyone to believe he does not exist!

However, whenever we watch a movie, when the congregation is gathered at the graveside, the one thing you will be sure to hear is the minister reading from the Book of Common Prayer: "Earth to earth, ashes to ashes, dust to dust; in sure and certain hope of the Resurrection into eternal life".

This actual sentence is not in the Bible, but it does sum up many verses which speak of 'the resurrection of the dead'. The fifteenth chapter of 1 Corinthians is called the 'resurrection chapter'. Here is an extract.

1 Corinthians 15:12 Now if Christ be preached that he rose from the dead, how say some among you that there is no resurrection of the dead? 13 But if there be no resurrection of the dead, then is Christ not risen: 14 And if Christ be not risen, then is our preaching vain, and your faith is also vain.

If you go to heaven when you die, what is the purpose of the resurrection?

If those now standing around the grave truly believe that the person in the coffin has actually gone to be with Jesus Christ in Heaven, we have a quandary. They must be in a state of perplexity, if he or she is in Heaven, and if they believe in the resurrection of the body, that is a puzzle.

If the person is now in Heaven with Christ, why would there need to be a resurrection? Would they come down from Heaven to Earth, get a new human body, then be changed into Immortality as they ascended once again to Heaven? That is not what happened to Jesus Christ.

1. He was alive.

2. He died on the cross and was put into a grave.

3. He was dead in the grave for three days and three nights.

4. He was then resurrected by God the Father to human life.

5. Then, He ascended to Heaven

6. In Heaven He was judged perfect, and was given Immortality by the Father.

7. Then He came back down to Earth to witness to His disciples.

8. Then in Acts it explains what Christ did before ascending to the Father

Acts 2:2 Until the day in which he was taken up, after that he through the Holy Ghost had given commandments unto the

apostles whom he had chosen: 3 To whom also he shewed himself alive after his passion by many infallible proofs, being seen of them forty days, and speaking of the things pertaining to the kingdom of God:

So what happens when a person dies? They die.
They cease to exist, and their spirit with all their life events recorded on it returns to God to be kept until that person is resurrected.

When they are resurrected, they are given a new human body, with their breath of life and their spirit, and they are alive again.

If they were living the life of a true Christian when they died, they will rise to meet Christ in the air, and be clothed with Immortality. This will also happen to true Christians who are alive at the time Christ returns. That is the glorious future for those who attain to the first resurrection.

Those who have not come to know Christ, and have not been converted, and have never had a chance to understand the Gospel will have to wait until the second resurrection.

Whenever that is for that person, they will be resurrected to human life, and given an opportunity to review their lives and their errors, and then be granted the gifts of belief, faith and repentance, and will begin to live as a Christian. At their maturity as a Christian, they will be changed and give Immortality.

But what about Hell, Purgatory, Limbo?
There are words usually translated Hell in the Bible. The word Sheol, which is a Hebrew word used for the abode of the dead. It is thought of as a place situated below the ground, the grave.

Ezekiel 31:15 Thus saith the Lord GOD; In the day when he went down to the grave I caused a mourning.

In the New Testament, the word 'tartarus' appears only once 'gehenna' several times.

2 Peter 2:4 God spared not the angels that sinned, but cast them down to hell [Tartarus], and delivered them into chains of darkness, to be reserved unto judgment.

This verse says that "the angels that sinned" aren't burning right now, and they certainly aren't suffering somewhere far beneath the earth. Tartarus means "dark abyss" or "place of restraint." It isn't a place of punishment either. It says Satan's angels are "reserved unto judgment," which means their punishment is yet future.

Gehenna was the narrow, rocky valley of Hinnom just south of Jerusalem where trash, filth, and the bodies of dead animals were burned up in Bible days. Historically this particular valley outside Jerusalem, was where children were sacrificed to the god Moloch.

Jeremiah 32:35 And they built the high places of Baal, which are in the valley of the son of Hinnom, to cause their sons and their daughters to pass through the fire unto Molech; which I commanded them not, neither came it into my mind, that they should do this abomination, to cause Judah to sin.

In later Jewish traditions Gehenna came to be associated with a place of torment and unquenchable fire that was to be the punishment for sinners. This is another doctrine of men.

Jesus Christ spoke about Gehenna many times such as in Matthew 5:22, 29, 30 where He warned about "the danger of hell (Gehenna) fire". Gehenna definitely suggests real flames. Christ shows us when the fire will burn:

Matthew 13:39 The enemy that sowed them is the devil; the harvest is the end of the world; and the reapers are the angels. As therefore the tares are gathered and burned in the fire; so shall it be in the end of this world. 41 The Son of man shall send forth his angels, and they shall gather out of his kingdom all things that offend, and them which do iniquity; 42 And shall cast them into a furnace of fire: there shall be wailing and gnashing of teeth.

Christ is describing a one time future event which will occur at the end of the age. He is not talking about a 'hell fire' to which everyone goes to in order to be eternally punished. We always need to keep in mind that many Scriptures are symbolic and figurative, as well as literal.

The pagan idea of Purgatory began creeping into the Catholic Church around the end of the sixth century, and they claim that this verse in Corinthians supports their view.

1 Corinthians 3:15 If any man's work shall be burned, he shall suffer loss: but he himself shall be saved; yet so as by fire.

However, this interpretation of 'Purgatory' is not consistent with other parts of the Holy Bible. Psalm 49 says tells us that a person cannot redeem a loved one, even if such a place did exist:

Psalm 49:6-7 They that trust in their wealth, and boast themselves in the multitude of their riches; None of them can by any means redeem his brother, nor give to God a ransom for him:

Purgatory as a doctrine teaches that a Christian's soul must burn in purgatory after death until all of their sins have been purged. To speed up the purging process, in earlier centuries, money could be paid to a priest so he could pray and have special masses for an earlier release, and much money was made with this doctrine.

Purgatory is given as a way that no matter how sinful or unbelieving, when you die, you go to Purgatory and get things sorted out and finally get to heaven, so no acceptance of Christ is needed, you can buy your way in.

Purgatory is given as an intermediate state, whereby minor sins may be absolved, and the person allowed eventually to enter heaven. This notion would not be necessary if Catholics truly believed that Christ's death effected absolution for all sin. However, Catholics do not believe that Christ's sacrifice on its own is sufficient, but believe that it is also necessary for a person to be in in a state of sacrimental grace in order to go to heaven. This is a form of works based salvation which is against God's Plan.

'Churchianity' absorbed the story of Dante's Inferno, a 14th-century poem, which also talked of the levels of Inferno fire, and Purgatory, as part of their desire to control people through fear. It tells of the fictitious journey of Dante through Hell, which is depicted as nine concentric circles of torment located within the Earth. It was thought to be the realm of those who have rejected spiritual values. It has been a part of most people's doctrinal beliefs in 'Christian' countries ever since.

It also formed part of the Greek pagan traditions, and their ideas were picked up by Hellenistic Jews. Sheol began to be compared to Hades of Greek mythology to refer to the abode of the dead, when they spoke of death, the grave, or the judgement, and later absorbed by newcomers to the Christian religion.

'Purgatory', is said to be a place to work out the result of evil works. Millions of Roman Catholics still think 'Purgatory' is place the dead go to be purified before entering heaven.

Why is it so vital that Christians believe God's Word on the subject of death?

As has been explained, this book is based on the fact that the Holy Bible is the Word of God, and that the original manuscripts are accurate in every detail. The Bible is truly God speaking to us today, through Christ and the Power of the Holy Spirit, and the Prophets, Disciples and Apostles.

Men did not write the Bible, yes, Christ as the Word of the Old Testament inspired the writers, and dictated every word to them for them to write down, no doubt working through their minds and allowing them to express their own person-alities without distorting His Truth.

Yes, all translations have their inaccuracies, but with a little research this can easily be overcome by the person who is asking God to teach them.

How to approach the Bible with faith and belief.

The Dr. Ernest Martin I mentioned earlier who spent many years in Biblical research gave a useful illustration that will help us to approach to the Bible in the right way. If we take two identical Bibles off the shelf, and place one on the left and one on the right side of the desk. You would think that they were both the Word of God, and you would be right.

If we start reading the Bible on the right, and believe ab-solutely what God says on the page, the rest of the Bible, all the way to the book of Revelation will tell us truths that make absolute sense and that you can rely on.

However if you look at the Bible on the left, and begin to study it, and you make the initial mistake in your approach to the Bible of not relying on God, but decide for yourself what you think it might mean you are in serious trouble.

Especially when you read the story in Genesis what the serpent says to Eve, and believe that concept "you will not die", then every word to the end of the book of Revelation will be contaminated with the teachings of the Devil, especially if you give heed to the serpent's lying teaching relative to the subject of death.

This is so important, it is impossible to emphasise enough just how important this is. Two identical Bibles, both the Word of God, and if you interpret or take on board what the serpent said instead of believing what God said, you have Satan's Bible.

If you read the other Bible and you believe every Word God says, then you have God's teaching all the way to the end of the Book.

Christians must believe that death means death.
The importance of understanding that death is death, the corpse of a person is as dead as a doornail, has ceased to exist, and has no consciousness, is an absolute bedrock belief for all Christians. Why?

Because if the Son of God who gave up His position in the God Family to become a man so that He could die and save us from our sin, and present us to His Father spotless and worthy to receive eternal life, if Christ did not die, then we do not have a Saviour, and we have no hope.

1 Corinthians 15:12 Now if Christ be preached that he rose from the dead, how say some among you that there is no resurrection of the dead? 13 But if there be no resurrection of the dead, then is Christ not risen: 14 And if Christ be not risen, then is our preaching vain, and your faith is also vain.

That is how important it is for all who would be Christians to understand that the doctrine of the "Immortality of the Soul" and "Reincarnation" are totally and completely incorrect.

God Created Adam

Genesis 2:7 And the LORD God formed man of the dust of the ground, and breathed into his nostrils the breath of life; and man became a living soul or creature.

This verse defines what the English word 'soul' means.

DUST + BREATH OF LIFE = LIVING 'Conscious' SOUL

A 'soul' is a person who has the gift of life from God until that person dies.

SOUL - BREATH = UNCONSCIOUS DEATH

As God breathed life into the man, He also breathed into him the 'human spirit' which enlivens the mind, and gives it the capacity to know and understand. When a person dies, the body turns back into 'dust', and the 'essence' of life and the spirit returns to God.

Ecclesiastes 12:7 Then shall the dust return to the earth as it was: and the spirit shall return unto God who gave it.

LIFE – BREATH - SPIRIT = UNCONSCIOUS DEATH

When a person is dead, they have ceased to exist in any conscious form.

Psalm 146:4 His breath goeth forth, he returneth to his earth; in that very day his thoughts perish.

Not only that, but all memories cease as the brain is dead.

Psalm 6:5 For in death there is no remembrance of thee: in the grave who shall give thee thanks?

So when we die, the breath of life leaves us. Our human spirit returns to God for safe keeping until the resurrection, when it will be reinstalled into our new body.

Ecclesiastes 12:7 Then shall the *dust* **return** *to the ea*rth as it was: and the spirit shall **return** unto God who gave it.

As Christians, part of our love for God is to give Him thanks continually while we are alive. And what is more, make the best of every moment while we are able.

Ecclesiastes 9:10 Whatsoever thy hand findeth to do, do it with thy might; for there is no work, nor device, nor knowledge, nor wisdom, in the grave, whither thou goest.

The lie about life after death began in the Garden of Eden
So God created Adam, and placed him in a garden.

Genesis 2:8 And the LORD God planted a garden eastward in Eden; and there he put the man whom he had formed.

In that very beautiful garden were many actual trees, and two particular fruit trees which also had both a figurative and symbolic meaning.

Genesis 2:9 And out of the ground made the LORD God to grow every tree that is pleasant to the sight, and good for food; the tree of life also in the midst of the garden, and the tree of knowledge of good and evil.

Many fruit trees, and two special trees, the 'Tree of Life' represented Eternal Life, and the tree of the 'Knowledge of Good and Evil'.

Genesis 2:16 And the LORD God commanded the man, saying, Of every tree of the garden thou mayest freely eat:

God told Adam that he may freely eat of every tree in the garden which must include the 'Tree of Life'; but God commanded Adam that there was one tree, (only one) that he may not eat on pain of death.

Genesis 2:17 But of the tree of the knowledge of good and evil, thou shalt not eat of it: for in the day that thou eatest thereof thou shalt surely die.

God gave a very specific command to Adam right from the beginning. Do NOT eat of the 'Tree of the Knowledge of Good and Evil' because if you do, you will die.

God then said that it was not good for Adam to be alone, and He would make a helpmate for him.

Genesis 2:18 And the LORD God said, It is not good that the man should be alone; I will make him an help meet for him.

Then the Bible tells how that after God had formed all the animals and birds, He brought them to Adam to name them, which he did.

Genesis 2:20 And Adam gave names to all cattle, and to the fowl of the air, and to every beast of the field; but for Adam there was not found an help meet for him.

But among all the creatures God had made, there was not a 'help meet', old English for a 'suitable' helper for Adam, so God put him to sleep, and made Eve.

Genesis 2:21 And the LORD God caused a deep sleep to fall upon Adam, and he slept: and he took one of his ribs, and closed up the flesh instead thereof; 22 And the rib, which the LORD God had taken from man, made he a woman, and brought her unto the man. 23 And Adam said, This is now bone of my bones, and flesh of my flesh: she shall be called Woman, because she was taken out of Man.

It is clear that God took the time to explain a lot of things to Adam and Eve, including the concept of marriage, important sexual details, and about the matter of procreation.

Genesis 2:24 Therefore shall a man leave his father and his mother, and shall cleave unto his wife: and they shall be one flesh. 25 And they were both naked, the man and his wife, and were not ashamed.

They had no reason to be ashamed of their nakedness. But Satan quickly sowed a guilty seed in their minds.

Genesis 3:7 And the eyes of them both were opened, and they knew that they were naked; and they sewed fig leaves together, and made themselves aprons.

But God took a different view and in verse 21, it tells how God clothed them, and made them beautiful coats of skins.

Their bodies were perfection personified, God saw to that. That ends the first part of the story of their life.

Enter the Biggest Lie! Eve's dialogue with the serpent.
In the next chapter of Genesis, we read the dialogue between God and Eve, and Satan and Eve in relation to death. The story begins with Eve on her own in the garden, when the subtle serpent comes to her, and talks to her.

Genesis 3:1 Now the serpent was more subtil than any beast of the field which the LORD God had made. And he said unto the woman, Yea, hath God said, Ye shall not eat of every tree of the garden?

The first thing that the serpent does is to question Eve about God's command concerning the trees, but it is clear that the serpent knew exactly what God had told Adam. One can almost hear the sarcasm in the manner in which the serpent poses the question to Eve.

Eve clearly knew the details of God's commandment and quoted what God had said to Adam before Eve had been formed. So Adam must have told her what God had said, no doubt in no uncertain terms. So Eve answers the serpent.

Genesis 3:2 And the woman said unto the serpent, We may eat of the fruit of the trees of the garden: 3 But of the fruit of the tree which is in the midst of the garden, God hath said, Ye shall not eat of it, neither shall ye touch it, lest ye die.

Eve is quoting what she knew that God had told her husband. The serpent's immediate response is flatly to contradict God's statement.

*Genesis 3:4 And the serpent said unto the woman, "**Ye shall not surely die**":*

This is the first and Biggest Lie contained in the Biblical narrative.

The serpent continues with his persuasive sales pitch. He tells Eve that when (not if) she eats the fruit, (it does not say apple or which fruit) she will suddenly have knowledge and understanding that will make her like a god.

Genesis 3:5 For God doth know that in the day ye eat thereof, then your eyes shall be opened, and ye shall be as 'gods', knowing good and evil.

So what was the serpent selling? He was subtly selling knowledge and a bright appealing future as a 'god' in order to get Eve to disobey God.

Genesis 3:6 And when the woman saw that the tree was good for food, and that it was pleasant to the eyes, and a tree to be desired to make one wise, she took of the fruit thereof, and did eat, and gave also unto her husband with her; and he did eat.

Adam took more notice of what Eve wanted to do, rather than obey God.

Genesis 3:7 And the eyes of them both were opened, and they knew that they were naked; and they sewed fig leaves together, and made themselves aprons.

So the knowledge that the serpent had promised, included Adam and Eve becoming aware of being naked, and being ashamed of that. Unfortunately, human beings have misused and defiled everything to do with sex, and Satan makes everyone feel at some level that sex is dirty and something to be ashamed of ever since.

Adam and Eve were in no doubt that they had done wrong, they had disobeyed God, and were very afraid of the consequences. So they hid themselves, and then they heard God calling out to them.

Genesis 3:9 And the LORD God called unto Adam, and said unto him, Where art thou? 10 And he said, I heard thy voice in the garden, and I was afraid, because I was naked; and I hid myself. 11 And he said, Who told thee that thou wast naked? Hast thou eaten of the tree, whereof I commanded thee that thou shouldest not eat? 12 And the man said, The woman whom thou gavest to be with me, she gave me of the tree, and I did eat.

The tendency in human nature is to attempt to avoid responsibility for our actions, and blame someone else. Not a happy trait. But God speaks to Eve.

Genesis 3:13 And the LORD God said unto the woman, What is this that thou hast done? And the woman said, The serpent beguiled me, and I did eat.

God told Eve that as a result of her rebellion against God, she would experience sorrow in childbearing. Then God says to Adam:

Genesis 3:17 And unto Adam he said, Because thou hast hearkened unto the voice of thy wife, and hast eaten of the tree, of which I commanded thee, saying, Thou shalt not eat of it: cursed is the ground for thy sake; in sorrow shalt thou eat of it all the days of thy life; 18 Thorns also and thistles shall it bring forth to thee; and thou shalt eat the herb of the field; 19 In the sweat of thy face shalt thou eat bread, till thou return unto the ground; for out of it wast thou taken: for dust thou art, and unto dust shalt thou return.

So for all time, men have had to deal with the curse God put on the land. Also here is God's clear statement about death, for dust thou art, and when you die, to dust you shall return.

The Doctrine of the 'Immortality of the Soul' is SATANIC

The serpent said, "You shall not die". This was Satan's teaching that when you die, you do not die completely, but part of you lives on as an immortal being.

Almost the whole world has gone after this Devilish teaching, "you will not die". Practically everyone in the world does not believe that when we die we cease to live or exist, but that a 'part' of us, the 'soul' or the 'spirit', or an 'essence' lives on.

This subject is very extremely serious as indeed it involves the first teaching God gave to Adam and Eve in the Book of Genesis in the Garden of Eden concerning His directives to them. So here is repetition for emphasis. God said:

Genesis 3:3 But of the fruit of the tree which is in the midst of the garden, God hath said, Ye shall not eat of it, neither shall ye touch it, lest ye die.

The lying serpent, (a symbol of Satan, that old Dragon that deceives the whole world) is the devil.

*John 8:44 **When he speaketh a lie, he speaketh of his own: for he is a liar, and the father of it.**)*

Satan called God a liar, accused God of lying! Then contradicted what God had said, when the Serpent said,

Genesis 3:4 And the serpent said unto the woman, Ye shall not surely die: *For God doth know that in the day ye eat thereof, then your eyes shall be opened, and ye shall be as gods, knowing good and evil.*

Satan's doctrine was that God had lied, as the Serpent here is teaching Eve that we do not die. If a person is a believer in the Bible, and believes that lie, then every verse to the end of Revelation in relation to death will be viewed by them through that lie. Satan will have achieved his plan of deceiving everyone who follows his teaching. The Bible interprets the Bible, the serpent is none other than Satan.

Revelation 12:9 And the great dragon was cast out, that old serpent, called the Devil, and Satan, which deceiveth the whole world: he was cast out into the earth, and his angels were cast out with him.

Of the up to two billion people who claim to follow Christian beliefs, most think that when we die we go to heaven. Many people assume that this belief is also a biblical belief, but is it? Emphatically NO!

What about all those billions on Earth who do not believe that the Holy Bible is God's Word? Almost all the world's religions and philosophies embrace some form of this falsehood that when a person dies, part of that person lives on.

So-called 'New Age' people and also many religions teach 'Reincarnation', and that after death, a soul or some part of the person within us, leaves the body and lives on for eternity during several 'incarnations' to a life back here on Earth.

What exactly is the history of this worldwide idea? We know from God's Word it began in the Garden of Eden. It was also believed by many of the nations before the flood.

The Egyptians from ancient times, believed strongly in the afterlife, and so they mummified their kings, the Pharaohs, and even millions of their pet dogs and cats. They put into their tombs all the things they felt would be necessary for them to enjoy in their next life.

The idea of the immortality of the soul was also a feature of the culture of the Greek philosophers in the 4th Century B.C. Later in the 1st Century A.D., this concept was prevalent, and those who believed it found it hard to let those ideas go as they became new Christians.

However, whether a person believes that the Bible is God's Word or not, God made the statement that if His human children broke his rule of law not to touch the Tree of Life then they would die. Be certain, Adam and Eve did die that day when they took of forbidden tree, they died spiritually that day, and they also died physically *within* God's 'day' of a thousand years.

Genesis 5:5 And all the days that Adam lived were nine hundred and thirty years: and he died.

Psalm 90:4 For a thousand years in thy sight are but as yesterday when it is past, and as a watch in the night.

2 Peter 3:8 But, beloved, be not ignorant of this one thing, that one day is with the Lord as a thousand years, and a thousand years as one day.

Adam and Eve 'died' when they took of the tree that God had said do not eat of it.

Genesis 3:3 But of the fruit of the tree which is in the midst of the garden, God hath said, Ye shall not eat of it, neither shall ye touch it, lest ye die.'

Protestants often refer to this event as 'the fall', the fall from Grace, and 'the fall' from God. When God formed Adam and Eve from the dust of the ground and breathed human spirit life into them, they also may have had the Holy Spirit at first. But when they disobeyed God and took of the tree of the knowledge of Good and Evil, and ate it, God took His Holy Spirit from them.

When the Holy Spirit is taken from a person that person dies spiritually. Nine hundred and thirty years later, within God's 'year', God took back his human spirit, and Adam died physically. God does not lie.

Hebrews 6:18 That by two immutable things, in which it was impossible for God to lie, we might have a strong consolation, who have fled for refuge to lay hold upon the hope set before us:

So all human beings can die spiritually if the Holy Spirit is taken from us, and certainly we all die physically. Human Beings have a human spirit which elevates our consciousness to be able to be aware of the God-Plane. This human (Hu – god, man) spirit is given to us with our first breath; and God takes it from us when we die physically.

Let us ask ourselves this question – what is it that we want saved? The flesh or the 'inner man'? It is our 'inner man', our spirit that holds the record of our entire life that we want saved! That is why it returns to God for safe keeping when we die.

While we are alive there is a silver cord (a symbol) which is the spiritual connection to us through which God channels His Power of Life to us by the flow of the Holy Spirit. When we die, that 'silver cord' is broken (symbolically) and the spirit returns to God.

Ecclesiastes 12:6 Or ever the silver cord be loosed, or the golden bowl be broken, or the pitcher be broken at the fountain, or the wheel broken at the cistern.

In this chapter where Solomon is talking about getting old, this verse 6 in poetic language is understood by some commentators to refer to the heart breaking down as we die.

Ecclesiastes 12:7 Then shall the dust return to the earth as it was: and the spirit shall return unto God who gave it.

To repeat for emphasis, God stores the human spirit of every person, and retains it until the day of our resurrection when that spirit is put into a new human body, which at that person's due time will change into a Spirit body.

That human spirit retains the imprint of everything that a person ever experiences, and every detail of their lives. We have a physical type of example of this in a CD, an MP3 file, or a DVD. All the information of this book is stored in a computer file on a disc. That type of information is not active, has no 'life', and cannot be 'read' without a machine designed to do that like a DVD player or a computer. It is the same with the human spirit.

Without a body, our human spirit has no consciousness, no life, no awareness of any kind, and no knowledge of all the information stored in it. Unless the human spirit is in a body ('machine') with a spirit enlivened mind to translate that information, it is lifeless. God can recognise each and every person by their unique DNA if by no other way.

God tells us: *When we are dead, we are completely dead!*

We can say, that is my house, or that is my car, or that is my spirit, but in reality all those things belong to God and are His. Our spirit keeps us alive, and motivates our every breath and our every heartbeat.

One has only to nibble, and mentally 'eat' a little bit at the serpent's statement, *'Ye shall not surely die',* like Eve and Adam did, and even give it any consideration at all you are on a certain path to being deceived by the master deceiver.

From then on, you will begin to read that lie into every verse about life and death in the Bible. You will take words which say you are going to die, and you are 'dead', completely dead, you are going to say, 'Oh no, that is not what those words mean'.

Possibly two billion people who think they are Christians do this, and think they go to heaven when they die. Their ministers teach it, and reinforce the same lie to each other, and soon they all believe that only the body dies, and the 'spirit' in some form lives on in heaven.

*Jeremiah 5:30 A wonderful and horrible thing is committed in the land; 31 The prophets (and priests, and ministers, and rabbis) prophesy falsely, and the priests bear rule by their means; and **my people love to have it so**: and what will ye do in the end thereof?*

Christians who have a fervent belief in this lie are often very happy with the concept. They love their 'churches', they love the comfort of having all those around them believing that you go to heaven when you 'die', and live a blissful life there. Our glorious future is so much better than that!

1 Corinthians 2:9 But as it is written, Eye hath not seen, nor ear heard, neither have entered into the heart of man, the things which God hath prepared for them that love him.

The tragedy is that so many are in love with a lie. Jesus states clearly in the Bible:

*John 3:12 If I have told you earthly things, and ye believe not, how shall ye believe, if I tell you of heavenly things? 13 And **no man hath ascended up to heaven**, but he that came down from heaven, even the Son of man which is in heaven.*

It is hard to credit, but people in general love to believe lies!

*Jeremiah 5:31 The prophets prophesy falsely, and the priests bear rule by their means; and **my people love** to have it so: and what will ye do in the end thereof?*

The time is coming before the second advent of Christ, when the whole world will be deluded.

*2 Thessalonians 2:9 Even him, whose coming is after the working of Satan with all power and signs and lying wonders, 10 And with all deceivableness of unrighteousness in them that perish; because they received not the love of the truth, that they might be saved. 11 **And for this cause God shall send them strong delusion, that they should believe a lie:** 12 That they all might be ~~damned~~ (*Strong's 2919 kreeno - determined or judged) who believed not the truth, but had pleasure in unrighteousness.*

Now here is the awful seriousness of this whole issue, when we come down to the time of Christ Jesus himself, He was sent into this world to fulfill a mission and *the* most important mission for you and for me, and for the whole world. Granted Christ's teaching was all both physical, figurative and symbolic. But Christ was totally committed to His mission and was willing to die up there on the tree of crucifixion to fulfill it. All that symbolism of His Birth, Life, Death and Resurrection are so very important.

If then we say, and believe that a part of man does not die, it follows that a part of Jesus did not die on the tree of crucifixion, that has to be so. People might say that His flesh died, almost everyone is willing to admit that, but they still think or believe that His 'inner man' did not die.

Here repeated for emphasis is this awesome fact that has to be faced by those who believe that part of us does not die is this:-

IF Christ's 'inner man', or His spirit did not die,

the sins of the whole world that were placed on Him have never yet been forgiven!

Everyone is still in their sins symbolically speaking!!

Some might say, 'Oh that is just foolishness'. They can say that, but it is not foolishness to those of us who trust the Scriptures, or to God. These important symbols are used in His teachings, and put in this form so that we can understand both them and God's plan for us all.

It is God's way to give us knowledge of Him, and the mission of Christ Jesus, and what we are going to be doing while here on Earth, and what is going to happen in the future. That is why these symbols are so very important.

So we need to look at the Biblical revelation, knowing and having proved to ourselves that the Bible is truly the Word of God, which states dogmatically and categorically that Christ *died* for our sins, and that He was resurrected the third day.

*1 Corinthians 15:3 For I delivered unto you first of all that which I also received, how that Christ **died** for our sins according to the scriptures; 4 And that he was buried, and that he rose again the third day according to the scriptures:*

Christ was resurrected from the dead,

not from any living activity,

because if He did not <u>die</u> for us, we do not have a Saviour.

BUT CHRIST JESUS DID DIE BOTH PHYSICALLY AND SPIRITUALLY SO WE COULD BE FORGIVEN AND SAVED FAULTLESS

But He did die, as it is possible for human beings to die, dead in all respects. Christ actually died two deaths on the tree.

One, He died spiritually when God the Father removed His Holy Spirit from Christ.

Matthew 27:46 And about the ninth hour Jesus cried with a loud voice, saying, Eli, Eli, lama sabachthani? that is to say, **My God, my God, why hast thou forsaken me?**

And secondly, a little while later when Christ died physically.

John 19:30 When Jesus therefore had received the vinegar, he said, **It is finished (His mission, the Work that God had given Him to do)**: *and he bowed his head, and gave up the* ~~ghost~~ *(Greek pneuma – physical breath, figuratively spirit, life).*

We need to realise that the Holy Spirit which Christ had had from birth, was taken from Him by His Father at almost the last moment of His life in order to fulfill the scripture that He would die so that we do not have to die.

God's Spirit was taken away so that He could die as a man and atone for all the ghastly, horrible, appalling, atrocious, execrable sins humankind had committed up to that time, and would ever commit in the future. Of course this is couched in symbolic terms, but we need to understand the horrendous yet wonderful facts those symbols represent.

Christ was Holy, Pure, Righteous, Sinless, and He is the only One who ever lived on this Earth that was 'good', but when those sins of ours and all of humanity, and even the sins of the spirit beings, were laid on His back and shoulders, Christ became 'sin' on that tree, accursed as Paul said, and was at that moment the most despicable man that epitomized 'sin' in all its forms. This was in the Plan of God and Christ from the beginning before the foundation of the world.

But of course in a true sense, in an actual sense, a moral sense, Christ was not in any way despicable at all, He was simply fulfilling His mission. Christ the Firstborn Son of God the Father who created all things, with all the Power of being part of the Godhead, was willing to give it up, become a man and present Himself as a sacrifice, to shed His blood, and die. This is why Christ's death was so powerful, because He had been willing to give up His place in the 'Father and Son Godhead' in order to save us from our sins. What manner of love was that?

Just before the crucifixion He prayed to the Father to give Him once again the glory that He had had before He willingly gave it up.

*John 17:5 And now, O Father, glorify thou me with thine own self with the **glory** which **I had with thee before the world was.***

What manner of love did the Father have for us?

John 3:16 For God so loved the world, that he gave his only begotten Son, that whosoever believeth in him should not perish, but have everlasting life. 17 For God (the Father) sent not his Son into the world to condemn the world; but that the world through him might be saved.

1 John 4:8 He that loveth not knoweth not God; for God is love.

To repeat for profound emphasis:

If Christ did not die, did not completely die, dead as a door-nail, for those three days in the tomb, then neither you, nor I, nor anyone has a Saviour. It is just that serious.

But He did die!!

He was resurrected from the dead as we saw in 1 Corinthians 15 above.

*John 20:16 Jesus saith unto her, Mary. She turned herself, and saith unto him, Rabboni; which is to say, Master. 17 Jesus saith unto her, Touch me not; for I am not yet ascended to my Father: but go to my brethren, and say unto them, I ascend unto my Father, and your Father; and to **my God, and your God**.*

Then He shortly went up to heaven to present Himself to the Father and to be judged. He was found to be a perfect sacrifice for sin and to be clothed with Immortality.

After that, He returned to the earth, and appeared to the Apostles for many days.

1 Corinthians 15:5 And that he was seen of Cephas, then of the twelve: 6 After that, he was seen of above five hundred brethren at once; of whom the greater part remain unto this present, but some are fallen asleep. 7 After that, he was seen of James; then of all the apostles. 8 And last of all he was seen of me also, as of one born out of due time.

He showed His disciples the nail marks in His hands, and the wound in His side, to prove that He was indeed the very One who was up there on that tree. This was absolutely ir-refutable evidence. Seeing all that clear evidence was what gave the disciples the courage and determination to go out and preach the Gospel of Jesus Christ, the Good News, to the whole world.

When Paul was in Athens in Greece, he went up to Mars hill, and met up with the Greek Philosophers there. They did not have access to the Scriptures, but part of their quest in life was to understand who 'God' was, who the 'Deity' was. They even had a monument to the 'Unknown God'.

Paul began to teach those Epicureans and Stoics, intelligent people, they spent their entire time talking about all kinds of imponderable questions and never coming to any real solid conclusions. They were "Ever learning, and never able to come to the knowledge of the truth", as Paul said of others.

While in Athens Paul began to teach about Christ Jesus, about the Gospel, and about that 'Unknown God' that they knew nothing about. All those learned people and philosophers listened as we can see in Acts 17.

Acts 17: 18 Then certain philosophers of the Epicureans, and of the Stoicks, encountered him. And some said, What will this babbler say? other some, He seemeth to be a setter forth of strange gods: because he preached unto them Jesus, and the resurrection. 19 And they took him, and brought him unto Areopagus, saying, May we know what this new doctrine, whereof thou speakest, is? 20 For thou bringest certain strange things to our ears: we would know therefore what these things mean. 21 (For all the Athenians and strangers which were there spent their time in nothing else, but either to tell, or to hear some new thing.) 22 Then Paul stood in the midst of Mars' hill, and said, Ye men of Athens, I perceive that in all things ye are too superstitious. 23 For as I passed by, and beheld your devotions, I found an altar with this inscription, TO THE UNKNOWN GOD. Whom therefore ye ignorantly worship, him declare I unto you.

It seems that these intellectual philosophers listened attentively to Paul as he expounded the Gospel, right up until he mentioned the resurrection, and then some of them laughed and jeered.

Acts 17:32 And when they heard of the resurrection of the dead, some mocked: and others said, We will hear thee again of this matter.

They could not believe such nonsense. From the dead? They mocked. They let Paul know in no uncertain terms that they **knew** that nobody actually dies, since they had all adopted the notion that part of a person does not die as part of their culture. But significantly, others in the crowd wanted to know more.

The crowd were saying to Paul, "Surely you know that nobody dies, part of a person lives on!! You understand about 'The Immortality of the Soul' don't you?" Virtually all the Greeks believed in the immortality of the soul. They thought that the very idea of 'resurrection' was foolishness, and this attitude is even more widespread worldwide in our 21st century era.

However though, the Greek crowd was not aware of the origin of this lying concept, and certainly did not know that it originated to begin with Satan the Devil in the Garden of Eden!

And now billions, perhaps a third of the world's population will say, yes we die physically, but there is a part of us that is immortal and never dies. This includes up to two billion people who claim to be, and think of themselves as 'Christian' who believe that they will go to heaven when they die, when the Bible clearly states that when they are dead they are **dead**.

The Fundamental Basis of Christianity.

The foundational belief of Christianity is that the man Christ, the human Son of God died on the tree of crucifixion and was resurrected from the dead.

It is fine to talk about and discuss with others who believe completely in the fact that the entire Bible is absolutely the inspired revelation of the Word of God, while understanding that there are errors of translation which can be easily resolved with earnest open minded study. Or as long as the conference is 'in Jerusalem' among believers, and not in 'Athens' with pagans, so to speak!

However it is not profitable to **debate**, or worse, argue with others who do not really believe that we have God's Word directly from Him. Or with people who take the Athenian Grecian philosophical view, who do not really believe in the inspiration of the revelation of the Bible. To 'debate' is listed with the fruits of the flesh.

And we would all relish the opportunity to be asked to talk about Christianity with anyone, believers or non-believers alike, as the Apostle Paul did. Discussions held in the right spirit can indeed be profitable as we strive to grow in grace and knowledge, but it is not good to enter into any type of discussion where a person, however sincere, might be attempting to convince us of their opinion.

A Christian is not interested in anyone's opinions, only in the statements of the inspired Word of God. A Christian should explain, yes, but also needs to be careful not to attempt to convince others of anything. When anyone asks, just enjoy telling them what the Bible teaches to the best of your ability.

In fact debating or arguing about doctrine, as was said above, is one of the fruits of the flesh.

*Romans 1:29 Being filled with all unrighteousness, fornication, wickedness, covetousness, maliciousness; full of envy, murder, **debate**, deceit, malignity; whisperers,*

The true Christian will always rely on Christ causing the flow of the Holy Spirit through their mind as they study and grow in grace, knowledge, and understanding.

We can all be very thankful that the Bible is so very clear about death, and that when we die we are dead, and will never need to get caught up in what almost the whole world believes.

John 8:31 Then said Jesus to those Jews which believed on him, If ye continue in my word, then are ye my disciples indeed; 32 And ye shall know the truth, and the truth shall make you free.

Jesus makes this promise to those who trust Him, that we shall be free of lies about Him.

*2 Corinthians 6:17 Wherefore come out from among them, and be ye **separate**, saith the Lord, and touch not the unclean thing (lies!); and I will receive you.*

We are to come apart and be separate from the world and all its so called 'attractions' and activities based on ancient pagan practices.

Our 'work' is to rejoice in having been given the opportunity to have this understanding to which so few have access.

CHAPTER 2

THE 2nd BIGGEST LIE - 'CHURCHIANITY'

There are thousands of denominations that call themselves 'Christian'

All have variations of teaching from the Bible. They cannot all be right! There is only ONE standard, ONE truth, directly from God's Word

BEWARE OF DECEPTION

*Matthew 24:4 And Jesus answered and said unto them, **Take heed that no man deceive you.** 5 For many shall come in my name, saying, I am Christ; and shall deceive many.*

God's Word uses repetition for emphasiss

*Luke 21:8 And he (Jesus Christ) said, Take heed that ye **be not deceived:** for many shall come in my name, saying, I am Christ; and the time draweth near: go ye not therefore after them.*

*Mark 13: 5 And Jesus answering them began to say, Take heed **lest any man deceive you:** 6 For many shall come in my name, saying, I am Christ; and shall deceive many.*

Luke 21: And he said, Take heed that ye **be not deceived:** for many shall come in my name, saying, I am Christ; and the time draweth near: go ye not therefore after them.

Any person who is deceived does not know they are.

Many organisations of men call themselves 'Churches of God', or God's Church, or similar names. Be assured the

Scriptures tell us very clearly that God is not running any organisation of men in our era, and He never did in the past. Jesus Christ is building His group, His ecclesia, and they are being given the opportunity to live **in** Him now and not on earth either.

Jeremiah 17:9 The heart is deceitful above all things, and desperately wicked: who can know it?

The mind of all human beings deceives itself, and is deceived by others who are deceptive by nature. We need to pray daily that we may be protected from deception of all kinds.

*2 Timothy 3:13 But evil men and seducers shall wax worse and worse, **deceiving, and being deceived**. 14 But continue thou in the things which thou hast learned and hast been assured of, knowing of whom thou hast learned them;*

Both Dr. Ernest Martin for decades, and I your author for nearly twenty years, were deceived by a deceitful man, who was preaching a counterfeit gospel. We were both convinced that we were part of the 'Work of God', and we absolutely believed that what we were taught by that organisation was the truth direct from the Bible.

It was not. Far from it, and we were totally deceived. Be warned. It can happen to anyone, when least expected.

Many years had to pass until God in His Mercy, revealed our error, and brought us to knowledge of His Truth. Be sure to check everything in this book carefully for yourself.

The Doctrine of the Trinity – Is it Biblical?
The historic mainstream body of Christian doctrine is not consistent with the Bible in many of its teachings. The 'Trinity" doctrine claims that the Creator God revealed in the Bible is eternally existent in three Persons. This is not

consistent with the Bible. It is a false doctrine believed by the majority of 'Churchianity'.

According to the Scriptures, the Godhead consists of the Father and His only begotten Son Jesus Christ. The Holy Spirit is the Manifestation of God's Power and is not a Person.

Access to Holy Spirit is given to Christians when they fulfill the conditions required to be a Christian. The Father and Christ impart knowledge, understanding, and wisdom by the flow of Holy Spirit in their minds. Without it, carnal minds are at enmity to God.

There is only one verse in the Bible that refers to a triune God, and it should not be there at all.

1 John 5:7 For there are three that bear record in heaven, the Father, the Word, and the Holy Ghost: and these three are one.

This scripture is well established to be spurious, in that is was added by men after the Canon of the New Testament was completed at the end of the 1st Century A.D.

Modern scholars, who have had access to collections of hundreds of manuscripts, are able to determine this verse was introduced into the Bible long after John wrote this letter. This verse is found in only eight late Greek

Manuscripts four of them have the words in a marginal note. Most of these Manuscripts originate from the sixteenth century.

It is an interesting to note that Paul in all his epistles never includes Holy Spirit in his greetings to the churches. If the Holy Spirit was a person and part of the Godhead, not to do so would be a form of blasphemy.

Romans 1:7 To all that be in Rome, beloved of God, called to be saints: Grace to you and peace from God our Father, and the Lord Jesus Christ.

Galatians 1:1 Paul, an apostle, (not of men, neither by man, but by Jesus Christ, and God the Father, who raised him from the dead;) 2 And all the brethren which are with me, unto the churches of Galatia: 3 Grace be to you

and peace from God the Father, and from our Lord Jesus Christ, 4 Who gave himself for our sins, that he might deliver us from this present evil world, according to the will of God and our Father:

Ephesians 1:1 Paul, an apostle of Jesus Christ by the will of God, to the saints which are at Ephesus, and to the faithful in Christ Jesus: 2 Grace be to you, and peace, from God our Father, and from the Lord Jesus Christ. 3 Blessed be the God and Father of our Lord Jesus Christ, who hath blessed us with all spiritual blessings in heavenly places in Christ:

We mention only three Epistles. Also James the brother of Christ says:

James 1:1 James, a servant of God and of the Lord Jesus Christ, to the twelve tribes which are scattered abroad, greeting.

Belief in the 'Trinity' suggests that the Godhead is a closed family unit. If this were true, it would deny the whole Purpose of God's Plan to increase His Family by bringing human beings to Glory as His Children.

Hebrews 2:9 But we see Jesus, who was made a little lower than the angels for the suffering of death, crowned with glory and honour; that he by the grace of God should taste death for every man. 10 For it became him, for whom are all things, and by whom are all things, in bringing many sons unto glory, to make the captain of their salvation perfect through sufferings.

The destiny of humans is to be given Eternal Life as a Gift from God to His Children, and live **in** Christ with Him.

John 3:16 For God so loved the world, that he gave his only begotten Son, that whosoever believeth in him should not perish, but have everlasting life. 17 For God sent not his Son into the world to condemn the world; but that the world through him might be saved.

FALSE CHRISTIANITY OR 'CHURCHIANITY'

The worldwide religion known as 'Christianity' has perhaps two billion believers. This currently includes Catholicism, many thousands of Protestant Groups, and Orthodox churches. All have their rituals and practices that are not Biblical, which have actually existed since the time of Nimrod who built the tower of Babel around 2160 B.C., if not before.

Paganism and heathen practices are still alive and well, and with us today. In a slightly different format yes, but with all the same elements that have existed for millennia.

Judges 21:25 In those days there was no king in Israel: every man did that which was right in his own eyes.

And the human race is still doing just that. Members of 'Churchianity' as a whole are 'doing their own thing', their own human thing, while true Christians are expected to be 'doing God's thing' but they are not!

Titus 1:16 They profess that they know God; but in works they deny him, being abominable, and disobedient, and unto every good work reprobate.

The reader does not have to take this author's word for anything, not for a moment. It is the simplest thing to go on to the Internet, and check each of the terms used, and statements made in this book.

WHAT MUST 21ST CENTURY CHRISTIANS AVOID LIKE THE PLAGUE? - IDOLATRY!

What does God say in His Word about idolatry?

Exodus 20: 3 Thou shalt have no other gods before me. 4 Thou shalt not make unto thee any graven image, or any likeness of any thing that is in heaven above, or that is in the earth beneath, or that is in the water under the earth.

Almost all churches around the world contain graven images, busts or statues purporting to be likenesses of Christ, Mary, angels, and 'saints'. Church buildings are adorned with demonic looking gargoyles and other stone images, and topped with steeples which were originally phallic symbols. Also 'likenesses' or pictures abound, 'relics' are preserved and adored in defiance of God's wishes and His Laws.

There is no doubt that the members of the early Church of false Christianity had already been practising many of the old idolatrous pagan customs for generations, and simply overlaid them with a Christian meaning to them.

IDOLATRY. Idolatry is one of the worst, if not the worst sin. Idolatry is mentioned in the Bible more times than any other human transgression.

God wants us to love and appreciate Him, to respect and honour Him, to hallow His name, and to avoid at all costs Spiritual fornication.

What are types of Idolatry or Spiritual fornication?

Just living our lives and ignoring God

Just living our lives, and consciously rejecting God as our Father.

Putting our focus on physical possessions and pleasures, money, and excluding God.

It is giving our love, time, energy, money, and attention to events, ideas, celebrations, or the observance of customs that have their roots in pagan and heathen worship of other gods.

Being part of this 'world' and all it offers, to the exclusion of loving God.

To give credit to 'Nature' or 'Evolution' for the amazing Creation instead of God.

Failing to Give God thanks and appreciation for life and every breath we breathe.

Britain, America, Canada, Australia, and most of the countries of Europe are referred to as 'Christian' countries. But are they? Historically, were the inhabitants of these countries truly God-fearing peoples? Or were they people who mostly practiced heathen, pagan ideas of worshipping the 'gods' as the majority of churchgoers do in our era?

Yet, these nations consider themselves as 'Christian' countries, and a high proportion of the citizens claim to be, or think of themselves as Christians, or at least 'nominal' Christians. Nominal Christians are Christians in name only, who may or may not actually attend a church or practice Biblical Christianity.

But, do these billions of people practice true Christianity, or what is taught in pagan riddled 'Churchianity'? The truth is that what is thought to be Christianity is giving God and Christ a bad name!! Ask anyone, and many will tell you, "It's religion that causes all the problems in the world!" And they have a point.

The word 'Churchianity' was coined to make a clear difference between those are 'nominal' (in name only) Christians, who just go through the motions in church services, and in their daily life; and those who are really committed 'True Christians?.

What does it mean to be a true Christian?

To be a committed Christians means to love God with all our mind, and His Word, the Holy Bible. Those Christian people who live by every Word of God as Jesus Christ commanded.

Matthew 4:4 But he (Christ Jesus) answered and said, It is written, Man shall not live by bread alone, but by every word that proceedeth out of the mouth of God.

Do the majority of churchgoers spend a good deal of time daily studying God's Word for Spiritual Food? Do they study for as much time as they spend eating physical food?

*Matthew 22:37 Jesus said unto him, Thou shalt **love the Lord thy God** with all **thy** heart, and with all **thy** soul, and with all **thy** mind.*

Luke 10:27 And he answering said, Thou shalt love the Lord thy God with all thy heart, and with all thy soul, and with all thy strength, and with all thy mind; and thy neighbour as thyself.

God uses repetition for emphasis. Do the majority of churchgoers really live the Christian life with all their heart, soul, mind, and strength? Or do they just practice a pleasant social life?

Men did not write the Bible! Yes, men physically put the marks on parchment, but it was Jesus Christ who inspired the writing of the entire Bible. Christ dictated word for word what was to be written down by His servants the Prophets, His Disciples, and His Apostles. The Bible is Truth, and is the only God-Inspired Guidebook for our lives on this earth.

From Genesis to Revelation, the Bible urges and commands us more than a hundred times to love God, and to keep His commandments and Laws.

Deuteronomy 7:9 Know therefore that the Lord thy God, he is God, the faithful God, which keepeth covenant and mercy with them that love him and keep his commandments to a thousand generations;

What defines a nominal 'Christian' in 'Churchianity'?
Those that say verbally that they are 'Christians', but the way they live their lives, and what they believe, proves that they are not. Christ speaks to them when He says:

Luke 6:46 And why call ye me, Lord, Lord, and do not the things which I say?

Billions who attend churches, whose ministers may use the name of 'Jesus' and 'Christ' all the time, but are in fact deceiving all those who are their congregations or adherents.

How can that be said about 'Christian' ministers? They seem to be so honest, and may appear to be, and perhaps are sincere people? But what does the Bible say about men and women who claim to be vicars of Christ? What does the word Vicar' mean?

The dictionary tells us: *vicar, early 14c., from Anglo-French vicare, Old French vicaire "deputy, second in command," also in the ecclesiastical sense, from Latin vicarius "a substitute, deputy, proxy," noun use of adjective vicarius "substituted, delegated," from vicis "change, interchange, succession; a place, position" (see vicarious). 'taking the place of another', The original notion is of "earthly representative of God or Christ.*

Can a mere human being be a 'substitute, a proxy, or a 'second in command', or 'take the place of' our Creator and Saviour, the Firstborn Son of God? Absolutely not! Can any human really 'forgive sins', or order 'penance' or 'absolution' of the penalty of sin? Of course not! That is naked sacrilege!

Any person who takes it upon themselves to hold any such position, in fact is deceiving themselves, is a deceitful person, and one who actually denies Christ. The Bible makes plain who and what they are.

2 Corinthians 11:13 For such are false apostles, deceitful workers, transforming themselves into the apostles of Christ. And no marvel; for Satan himself is transformed into an angel of light. Therefore it is no great thing if his ministers also be transformed as the ministers of righteousness; whose end shall be according to their works.

They may look impressive in their priestly garb, but do not be fooled. Many wear the 'fish' hats of Dagon the fish 'god'.

Matthew 15:8 his people draweth nigh unto me with their mouth, and honoureth me with their lips; but their heart is far from me. But in vain they do worship me, teaching for doctrines the commandments of men.

Such people are doing Satan's work by operating a 'counterfeit' system of Christianity. Hard words? They are not the words of this writer, but God's.

Beware deception and being deceived.
Matthew 24:4-6 And Jesus answered and said unto them, Take heed that no man deceive you. For many shall come in my name, saying, I am Christ; and shall deceive many.

We need to examine what we believe. Here repeated is an absolute truth which everyone needs to understand:

Anyone who is deceived does not know they are deceived.

Those who are deceived, and not aware of it, get involved with and practice lies, and are in fact being hypocritical without realising it.

2 Timothy 3:13 But evil men and seducers shall wax worse and worse, deceiving, and being deceived.

The only way anyone can find out it if they are deceived or not is to ask God for the 'eyes to see', and the 'ears to hear', and for the gift of repentance. Then to study God's Word, and compare what the Bible actually says with what they have been taught in seminaries and churches, and what they have allowed into their minds and practice in daily life as 'truth'.

Have regular churchgoers been deceived into thinking, be-lieving in and practicing activities based on paganism and ancient heathen idolatrous rites? YES! Do people who call themselves 'Christian' realise or appreciate that God HATES the traditional activities they engage in? NO!!

*1 Timothy 4:1 Now the Spirit speaketh expressly, that in the latter times some shall depart from the faith, giving heed to **seducing spirits**, and doctrines of devils;*

Which idolatrous activities are these? These teachings are an integral part of popular 'Churchianity':- Christmas, Lent, Easter, and Hallowe'en. There are also others observed in 'Churchianity' not mentioned here. These practices were all in existence thousands of years before Christ Jesus came into this world and created 'Christianity'.

But one might say, Christmas, Lent, Easter, Hallowe'en and other 'Christian' festivals are not bad. "Surely they are just harmless ways in which people choose to worship their idea of God?" Absolutely, if there is no Almighty God, but only those 'gods' they create in their own minds. What does God say about these activities in the Holy Bible? Later in this chapter each of these rituals of 'Churchianity' will be examined in detail.

What does the word 'Church' mean? And does it matter?

Firstly the English word 'church' is a word derived from the name of an ancient goddess whose name was 'Circe'. Who was 'Circe' and what type of 'god' was she?

Circe, pronounced Kirky, is the Greek word Kírke which gave rise to the Scottish and Welsh word 'Kirk' or 'church' still in common use today. The mythical Circe was said to be the daughter of the Sun god Helios. Anyone may observe that many church buildings are decorated with circular stained glass windows, and other designs that were historically used in Sun worship.

Circe, Kirkee, was a goddess of magic, a nymph, a witch, an enchantress or sorceress who used Pharmakeia which involved the administering of drugs, poisoning and magical arts in connection with her brand of idolatry.

Exodus 22:18 Thou shalt not suffer a witch to live.

Deuteronomy 18:10 There shall not be found among you any one that maketh his son or his daughter to pass through the fire, or that useth divination, or an observer of times, or an enchanter, or a witch.

Galatians 5:19 Now the works of the flesh are manifest, which are these; Adultery, fornication, uncleanness, lasciviousness, 20 Idolatry, witchcraft, hatred, variance, emulations, wrath, strife, seditions, heresies, 21 Envyings, murders, drunkenness, revellings, and such like: of the which I tell you before, as I have also told you in time past, that they which do such things shall not inherit the kingdom of God.

Circe was believed to use the magic of metamorphosis, changing men into animals. She had the power of illusion, and practiced the dark art of necromancy, the practice of communicating with the dead, in attempts to predict the future.

The majority of 'Churchianity' teaches and believes that when we die, we go to heaven. This leads some to claim they can contact dead people, necromancy, through mediums, the use of pendulums and other means. The Bible teaches that when a person dies, they are dead, and are not conscious in any way.

Ecclesiastes 9:5 For the living know that they shall die: but the dead know not any thing, neither have they any more a reward; for the memory of them is forgotten.

Incidentally, if Christ did not die, and lie in the grave dead for three days and three nights, we do not have a Saviour! But He did die.

So is the word 'church' an appropriate word to use in connection with Christ Jesus or Christianity, and the worship of the True God? No!

Language, the manner and way we use words is vitally important. We should use specific words to convey exact meanings to each other in spoken or written language.

In 1611 A.D., forty-seven scholarly translators under the direct instructions of King James of England were expressly told by the King not to translate any portion of the Bible in a manner which would go against or not support the doctrines of the Church of England. The King wanted to maintain his authority as the head of the church.

So the translators of the original Scripture manuscripts consistently translated the one hundred and eleven times the Greek word "ekklesia" appeared in the original manuscripts as 'Church' in the King James Version. Most other versions of the Bible have followed this pattern.

So the translators knowingly used the word 'Church' which means a 'building' to support a clergy; rather than the word 'ecclesia' meaning assembly, that would build a unified group of Christians, who are the 'body of Christ'.

The use of this one word 'Church' instead of 'ekklesia' has literally changed the world. Using the word "Church" in the Bible has implanted a completely wrong concept of Christ's body into the minds of those who believe in 'Churchianity'.

When Jesus said, *"Upon this rock I will build my ~~church~~ ekklesia."* (Mat 16:18) The Greek word in the original text is 'ekklesia' pronounced ek-klay-see-ah.

The dictionary definition of the word 'Church' is a 'building', a 'place of worship of any religion'. The actual definition of the Greek word "ekklesia" is 'group' or 'assembly'.

Incidentally, the early assembly of Christian believers in the 1st Century A.D. did not have ministers over the rest of the group. As 'Churches' began to develop, they became structured with an authoritarian hierarchy that needed buildings to control the people religiously and politically.

By changing the true meaning and function of the Greek word "ekklesia" to our English word "church", it gave the system of clergy power over the people. The fact that "power corrupts and absolute power corrupts absolutely" has been the downfall and corruption of original Christianity and of the entire 'Churchianity' system of tens of thousands of differing and divided denominations to this day.

21st Century 'Churchianity' keeps pagan idolatry alive and well

What does God say in the Bible about learning and practising the ways of the pagans and heathen nations? Should anyone incorporate any form of worship or any such practices into a form of Christianity?

*Deuteronomy 18: 9 When thou art come into the land which the Lord thy God giveth thee, **thou shalt not learn** to do after the abominations of those natio*ns.

What does God have to say in His Word about the various practices involved with the festive seasons or 'feasts' of Xmas, Lent, Easter, Halloe'en?

*Isaiah 1:13 Bring no more vain oblations; incense is an abomination unto me; the new moons and sabbaths, the calling of assemblies, I cannot away with; it is iniquity, even the solemn meeting. 14 Your new moons and **your appointed feasts my soul hateth**: they are a trouble unto me; I am weary to bear them. 15 And when ye spread forth your hands, I will hide mine eyes from you: yea, when ye make many prayers, I will not hear: your hands are full of blood. 16 Wash you, make you clean; put away the evil of your doings from before mine eyes; cease to do evil;*

God says to those who claim to be Christian, many things you sincerely believe, or think you are using to worship Me are vain, empty. And worse than that, God says 'I HATE THEM!'

Malachi 2:3 Behold, I will corrupt your seed, and spread dung upon your faces, even the dung of your solemn feasts; and one shall take you away with it.

So God hates it when His children use the ways of the heathen to worship Him. He calls any form of services like that 'dung', and what is more, would like to spread that manure on your faces. He cannot make it plainer than that!

Even in the face of such strong words from God, 'Churchianity' does not use the Bible as God's instruction for the way of life of the Christian, otherwise they would shun Xmas, Lent, Easter, Halloe'en like they would the Bubonic Plague!

The rituals of 'Churchianity' need to be exposed for what they really are.

Christmas – When was Jesus Christ really born?

Let this be absolutely clear, Christmas has absolutely nothing whatsoever to do with the birth of Christ. The Bible gives astronomical details which enabled Dr. Ernest L Martin to calculate and establish the time of Christ's birth to within forty-five minutes on September 11, 3 B.C.E. This calculation has been accepted as fact by top Astronomers and Planetariums around the world.

According to the Scriptures, Christ was born on the Holy Day, the Day of Trumpets, 3 B.C., which occurs annually on the 'Jewish' ecclesiastical (God's) calendar in the 1st of Tishri. This is around September in the Gregorian calendar the most widely used civil calendar worldwide since the decree of Pope Gregory XIII who introduced it in October 1582.

Christ was born during the reign of the Emperor Augustus (63 BC-AD 14), and the nation of Israel was under the control of the occupying Roman army. The Roman Empire at that time had many gods, and the most important was 'Saturn'. 'Saturnalia' originated as a farmer's festival in honour of Saturn (*satus* means sowing).

Initially, it was a two-day affair starting on December 17th. But later the festivities became a seven-day event. Changes to the Roman calendar moved the climax of Saturnalia to

December 25th, almost exactly the time of the date of the winter solstice when the days were shortest, and the Sun appeared to be lowest in the sky.

The festival of 'Saturnalia', also involved the worship of the Sun. It was about the 'death' and 'rebirth' of the Sun and celebrating the Sun's 'birthday' as the days began to get longer.

Christ's birth was a local affair in Bethlehem, and the actual date of his birth was lost to the average person of the time. As the growth of Christianity developed and reached the common people who all celebrated 'Saturnalia', and the 'birth' and 'death' of the Sun, they did not change their habits, just changed the emphasis in their minds.

So it is easy to see how the Birth and Death and Resurrection to life of Jesus Christ were easily absorbed by people who were used to the practice of Saturnalian festivities. All that was necessary was a change of name from 'Saturnalia' to 'Christmas', and they could carry on as they always had.

Nowadays that period is called 'Christmas' by one and all around the world.

'Saturnalia' was also celebrated around the 22nd to the 25th December according to the Gregorian calendar, the Winter solstice when the Sun was at its lowest in the sky, and began to appear to go upwards again. Of course this is due to the rotation of the Earth, rather than movement of the Sun.

After the shortest day, around the 24th December, each day would get a little longer, and those observing 'Saturnalia' began to celebrate the 'birthday' of the Sun. It is easy to see how people who were engrained in this practice, when they heard about the birth of Christ, it was a simple matter to attach His name to their festive season, and carry on much as before.

Public and commercial hysteria around the Christmas period now begins around October, continues in November, and consumes the attention and the finances of billions for weeks on end. Certainly nobody sees anything wrong with it. Most think it is all just harmless fun. But is it?

What does God have to say about it? Actually He hates the whole thing.

*Jeremiah 10:3 2 Thus saith the Lord, Learn **not** the way of the heathen, and be not dismayed at the signs of heaven; for the heathen are dismayed at them. 3 For the customs of the people are vain: for one cutteth a tree out of the forest, the work of the hands of the workman, with the axe. 4 They deck it with silver and with gold; they fasten it with nails and with hammers, that it move not.*

So Christmas trees may look pretty with their lights that picture the diminished light of the Sun, but they are an abomination to God, as is the practice of Sun worship or the worship of any material things.

Nimrod was a despot who built the Tower of Babel (Babylon) before the Flood. He wanted the nations to worship him as god, and so he built the tower 'up to heaven'.

An old fable of Babylon told of an evergreen tree which sprang out of a dead tree stump. The old stump symbolized the dead Nimrod. The new shoots on the evergreen tree symbolized that Nimrod had come to life again in Tammuz! The female god Isis was the mother figure (not Mary as some believe, but actually the 'Queen of Heaven') and gave birth to Tammuz.

It is easy to see how this symbolism concerning the death and rebirth of Tammuz or Nimrod, could have been adopted by those who first learned about the death and resurrection of

Christ. They could take up the 'new' religion of Christianity, and basically carry on as they had from time immemorial.

The use of an evergreen tree was to symbolise life, evergreen Holly with its bright red berries pictured the light of the sun. Evergreen plants formed the wreath hung on people's front doors represented mourning for the dying Sun. Strange that people still do this today, yet say they are thinking of the birth of Christ, not His death. How deeply engrained are the traditions people adhere to generation after generation.

Saturnalia had been practiced since time began; it was a time of debauchery, drunkenness, over eating, and the exchange of gifts. Christmas is a time when many of the works of the flesh occupy people's minds and activities. It is frequently reported that there is more domestic violence, sexual assaults, suicide, and crimes involving alcohol at Christmastime, than at any other time of the year.

Galatians 5:19 Now the works of the flesh are manifest, which are these; Adultery, fornication, uncleanness, lascivious-ness, 20 Idolatry, witchcraft, hatred, variance, emulations, wrath, strife, seditions, heresies, 21 Envyings, murders, drunkenness, revellings, and such like: of the which I tell you before, as I have also told you in time past, that they which do such things shall not inherit the kingdom of God.

The activities and excesses of people during the celebration of Christmas are neither Christian nor Godly.

Ezekiel 8:11 And there stood before them seventy men of the ancients of the house of Israel, and in the midst of them stood Jaazaniah the son of Shaphan, with every man his censer in his hand; and a thick cloud of incense went up. 12 Then said he unto me, Son of man, hast thou seen what the ancients of the house of Israel do in the dark, every man in the chambers of his imagery? for they say, the LORD seeth us not; the LORD hath forsaken the earth.

Interesting that incense is mentioned here as part of pagan worship. The scripture also mentions men with censers and a thick cloud of incense, a practice that continues in churches to this day. These rituals were performed in the gloom and dark of the temples of the gods, not unlike the dim light in some churches now.

Ezekiel 8:3 He said also unto me, Turn thee yet again, and thou shalt see greater abominations that they do. 14 Then he brought me to the door of the gate of the LORD's house which was toward the north; and, behold, there sat women weeping for Tammuz (Nimrod, Santa Claus!)

In London, England, it is an extraordinary fact is that the source or origin of the River Thames (pronounced 'Temmes' or Tammuz?) is the River Isis. Isis was the mother of Tammuz. So the River 'Isis' flows into and gives rise to, or gives birth to the Tammuz or Thames. It is incredible how over thousands of years so many of the pagan myths have persisted and are still with us today.

What about Santa Claus?
According to *some historians*, "Santa" was a common name for Nimrod throughout Asia Minor. God forbade the worship of any god before Him, but Nimrod had exalted himself, built the tower of Babel, and sought the worship of the people. So God destroyed the tower and confused the one language of the nations to slow down their ability to make human progress into more evil, and for a lesson to any man who would think to be worshipped as god.

Genesis 11:1 And the whole earth was of one language, and of one speech... 6 And the LORD said, Behold, the people is one, and they have all one language; and this they begin to do: and now nothing will be restrained from them, which they have imagined to do. 7 Go to, let us go down, and there confound their language, that they may not understand one another's speech.

Nimrod was also the fire god who supposedly came down the chimneys of the ancient pagans. People still perpetuate and teach their children the myth, the lie that Santa comes down the chimney with gifts. How strange is that?

The same fire god to whom infants were burned and eaten in human sacrifice was a practice among those who were once God's people. Of course babies and infants are not burned and eaten today, but millions of babies are killed and aborted, sacrificed to the desires and whims of many cultures to the 'god' of selfishness.

Today Santa Claus derives from Saint Nicholas. 'Ho! Ho! Ho! Jolly Old Nick' or 'Santa' may seem to be fun, but it is another term used to refer to the devil.

*Revelation 2:6 tells about the church that has the "doctrine of the Nicolaitanes," which Christ twice tells His Church **He hates**.*

The word Nicolaitane means "follower of Nicholas." *Nikos* means 'destroyer'. *Laos* means 'people.' Nicolaitanes, then, are people who follow the ideas of the destroyer – Nimrod who, in his own mind, elevated himself above God.

*Genesis 10:9 He was a mighty hunter **before the Lord**: wherefore it is said, Even as Nimrod the mighty hunter before the Lord.*

Before: Strong's 6440 μυnip; — paniym, paw-neem'; plural (but always as singular). against, anger, + impudent

Those who believe that following Christmas is an innocent Christian custom will be astonished when they discover where it all originated, and that Christ hates the whole practice. But will that change the way they think?

What about the 'Nativity' scenes and plays in churches?

As a matter of accuracy, what does the Bible say about the birth of Christ? Why was He born in a stable? Were Mary and Joseph poor? When was He born? In that time, shepherds were never in the fields in December in the Jerusalem area!

What about the Kings of the Orient and the Star? It certainly does not say there were three kings, nor that they gave presents to each other! They were not present in the stable with baby Jesus. When they first saw Him, he was a 'young child', not a baby, and the Bible account makes that clear many times.

The whole 'Christmas scene' pictured, and the 'Nativity play' performed in churches and hotels around the world give a completely false idea of what the Bible actually says about the detail of those events.

The reason Mary and Joseph were in a stable was because the occupying Roman officials had proclaimed a Census to get a head count of all the people from miles around, and collect taxes at the same time. This is a historical fact, not some idle story.

Luke 2:1 And it came to pass in those days, that there went out a decree from Caesar Augustus that all the world should be taxed. 2 (And this taxing was first made when Cyrenius was governor of Syria.) 3 And all went to be taxed, every one into his own city.

That was why there was no room in the Inn or any other place to stay. Mary and Joseph certainly were not poor, they were descendants of the Royal House of David, and were certainly well off.

Luke 2: 8 And there were in the same country shepherds abiding in the field, keeping watch over their flock by night.

The shepherds came down from the hills to see the baby because it was in September time, and the bad weather had not caused them to come down from the high country. They would not have still been out in the open in December.

Luke 2:9 And, lo, the angel of the Lord came upon them, and the glory of the Lord shone round about them: and they were sore afraid. 10 And the angel said unto them, Fear not: for, behold, I bring you good tidings of great joy, which shall be to all people. 11 For unto you is born this day in the city of David a Saviour, which is Christ the Lord. 12 And this shall be a sign unto you; Ye shall find the babe wrapped in swaddling clothes, lying in a manger.

The word 'babe' in the Greek is Strong's (1025) bre>fov, — bref'-os; an infant (properly unborn) literal or figurative: — babe, (young) child, infant. So how old was Jesus Christ when the shepherds visited Him? From the next part of the account in Luke, it is clear that Jesus had only just been born. The shepherds then went back up to the hills, and Jesus and his parents stayed in Jerusalem for at least eight days until He was circumcised.

This word 'brefos' translated 'babe' only appears twice in the stories about the birth of Christ, and the word 'paidi>on' translated 'young child appears six times in connection with the story of the wise men. God wrote the Bible, and He does not make mistakes!

Luke 2:16 And they (the shepherds) came with haste, and found Mary, and Joseph, and the babe (Gr. 'brefos' baby) lying in a manger.

Christ was born in a stable, and was put into the feeding trough for the animals which was called a manger. When we read of the visit of the wise men, they went 'into the house' to see the 'young child'.

Luke 2:20 And the shepherds returned, glorifying and prais-ing God for all the things that they had heard and seen, as it was told unto them. 21 And when eight days were ac-complished for the circumcising of the child, his name was called Jesus, which was so named of the angel before he was conceived in the womb.

The story of the visit of the wise men.

Now when looking at the account and details of the visit of the wise men, the Greek word *'pahdeon'* used to describe Jesus means young child, not baby.

Matthew 2:1 Now when Jesus was born in Bethlehem of Ju-daea in the days of Herod the king, behold, there came wise men from the east to Jerusalem, 2 Saying, Where is he that is born King of the Jews? for we have seen his star in the east, and are come to worship him. 3 When Herod the king had heard these things, he was troubled, and all Jerusalem with him. 4 And when he had gathered all the chief priests and scribes of the people together, he demanded of them where Christ should be born. 5 And they said unto him, In Bethle-hem of Judaea: for thus it is written by the prophet, 6 And thou Bethlehem, in the land of Juda, art not the least among the princes of Juda: for out of thee shall come a Governor, that shall rule my people Israel.

Herod wanted to find out exactly when Christ had been born, as he was planning to kill all the boy children who had been born around that time who might be a threat to him.

*Matthew 2:7 Then Herod, when he had privily called the wise men, enquired of them diligently what time the star appeared. 8 And he sent them to Bethlehem, and said, Go and search diligently for the **young child**; and when ye* *have found him, bring me word again, that I may come and worship him also. 9 When they had heard the king, they departed; and, lo, the star, which they saw in the east, went before them, till it came and stood over where the **young child** was.*

Notice here the inspired Scripture states that the wise men observed the Star which stood over where the **young child** was. It does not say 'baby', it says 'young child'.

The Greek word translated **'young child'** here (3813) paidi>on, — pahee-dee'-on; neuter diminative of (3816) (pai~v); a childling (of either sex), i.e. an infant, or (by extension) a half-grown boy or girl; figurative an immature Christian: — (little, young) child, damsel.

*Matthew 2:10 When they saw the star, they rejoiced with exceeding great joy. 11 And when they were come **into the house,** they saw the **young child** with Mary his mother, and fell down, and worshipped him: and when they had opened their treasures, they presented unto him gifts; gold, and frankincense and myrrh.*

The wise men brought three different categories of present yes, but nowhere does the Bible say how many wise men there were. Does this account matter? Yes. Notice also that the wise men came *into the house,* **not the stable!** Their visit was at a different time and a different place from when and where Christ was born.

The whole story of the event concerning Christ's birth is incorrectly presented by 'Churchianity' to billions all over the world. Jesus was not a baby when the wise men presented their gifts to Him, (not to each other!), He was a young child. This fact is repeated for emphasis again in verse 13. He was under two years old, but not a baby. As the wise men had explained to Herod exactly when the Star appeared, Herod ordered the massacre of all boy children under two years old in order to ensure that Christ was killed, but Joseph had been warned to flee to Egypt to avoid that.

*Matthew 2:12 And being warned of God in a dream that they should not return to Herod, they departed into their own country another way. 13 And when they were departed, behold, the angel of the Lord appeareth to Joseph in a dream, saying, Arise, and take the **young child** and his mother, and flee into Egypt, and be thou there until I bring thee word: for Herod will seek the **young child** to destroy him. 14 When he arose, he took the **young child** and his mother by night, and departed into Egypt: 15 And was there until the death of Herod: that it might be fulfilled which was spoken of the Lord by the prophet, saying, Out of Egypt have I called my son.*

Jesus Christ was taken to safety to Egypt by His parents by Divine Providence.

Matthew 2:16 Then Herod, when he saw that he was mocked of the wise men, was exceeding wroth, and sent forth, and slew all the children that were in Bethlehem, and in all the coasts thereof, from two years old and under, according to the time which he had diligently inquired of the wise men.

The Romans had no mercy, when it came to slaughtering all who might be a threat to their reign.

So it is clear, the Christmas story told in churches does not match the Biblical account at all! As it so often the case, so much of the information people learn in their association with 'Churchianity' about the birth of Christ, and for that matter about the entire Bible, bears little relationship to the detail God has inspired to be written in the Scriptures of the Holly Bible for our instruction.

Lent

The Etymological dictionary says: *"the word 'Lent' comes from an ancient word referring to the period between Ash Wednesday and Easter. Late 14c., short for Lenten (n.) "now the forty days of fasting before Easter" in the Christian calendar (early 12c.), from Old English lencten "springtime, spring," the season, also "the fast of Lent," from West Germanic *langitinaz "long-days," or "lengthening of the day" (source also of Old Saxon lentin, Middle Dutch lenten, Old High German lengizin manoth). This prehistoric compound probably refers to increasing daylight in spring."*

According to the Catholic Encyclopaedia, Lent was absorbed into the Catholic Church by St. Athanasius in 339 A.D., and its practice continues to this day.

Lent is now seen as a solemn religious observance in the 'Christian' liturgical calendar, or those events pertaining to worship or religious ceremonies, but its practices go back many centuries before Christ.

Figuratively, it is forty days, which in the Bible is typical of a period of trial. Forty is often a significant number for any event. For instance, Christ was in the desert fasting for forty days and nights before Satan came to test him.

However, Lent is not exactly forty days. It begins on Ash Wednesday and ends approximately six weeks later, before Easter Sunday. The proposed purpose of Lent is the preparation of the believer through prayer, doing penance, mortifying the flesh, repentance of sins, giving to charities, and self-denial.

These are all typical of spiritual matters that Christ performed for us, when He hung on the tree, and died for and paid for our sins. We cannot do penance for our sins, as Christ already did that for us. Yes we should repent of our sins daily, not just on a few weeks a year!! Self denial is achieved by asking God to help us to put Him first and ourselves second.

Easter

What about Easter? The English name Easter came from the Anglo-Saxon spring goddess Eostre or Ishtar. (Ishtar is the root of the English word for Estrogen a female sex hormone.) It is also connected to Astarte, the Phoenician fertility goddess, and the Babylonian chief goddess Ishtar.

Hares, rabbits, and eggs are symbols of fertility used in the ancient ceremonial and symbolism pagan spring festivals. The hunt for Easter eggs, supposedly brought by the Easter rabbit (!), far from being harmless child's play, originated in a pagan fertility rite. Some still believe that the decorated Easter egg can 'magically' bring happiness, prosperity, and health. The link between such things and sex is inescapable.

Easter sunrise services are clearly linked to rites of ancient Sun worshippers performed at the Vernal or Spring equinox. They worshipped and welcomed the Sun and its great power to bring new life to all growing things.

*Ezekiel 8:15 Then said he unto me, Hast thou seen this, O son of man? turn thee yet again, and thou shalt see **greater abominations** than these.16 And he brought me into the inner court of the LORD's house, and, behold, at the door of the temple of the LORD, between the porch and the altar, were about five and twenty men, with their backs toward the temple of the LORD, and their faces toward the east; and they worshipped the sun toward the east.*

Harmless? Not according to God's Word! God does not consider it a 'light' thing, that they are committing pagan abominations in the House of God.

Ezekiel 8:17 Then he said unto me, Hast thou seen this, O son of man? Is it a light thing to the house of Judah that they commit the abominations which they commit here? for they have filled the land with violence, and have returned to provoke me to anger: and, lo, they put the branch to their nose.

By doing so, they are putting a branch to God's nose. Ghastly! This figure of speech is continued in type to this day when rude children put their thumb to their noses in an insulting manner which exemplifies disrespect. Do 'Christians' realise that they are insulting God in this way when they go to a solemn Easter sunrise service? Of course not! But that does not alter the fact that is how God sees it. Frightening really!

The widespread worship of the sex goddess Ishtar (Easter) had its focus in the Springtime when all life was bursting forth. When Christianity began, it was a simple matter for people adopt and modify its ideas and to link these pagan practices to the worship of Christ who died and rose again in the Spring, and call it 'Easter'.

Jeremiah 44:19 And when we burned incense to the queen of heaven , and poured out drink offerings unto her, did we make her cakes (hot cross buns?) to worship her, and pour out drink offerings unto her, without our men?

The 'queen of heaven' referred to here is Ishtar ('Oestre', Goddess of sex and procreation, 'Easter', estrogen – a female sex hormone). Ishtar was an Assyrian and Babylonian goddess also called Ashtoreth and Astarte by various other groups. She was thought to be the wife of the false god Baal (the Sun god), also known as <u>Molech</u>.

The motivation of women to worship Ashtoreth stemmed from her reputation as a fertility goddess, and, as the bearing of children was greatly desired among women of that era, worship of this "queen of heaven" was rampant among pagan civilizations. This idolatrous practice had also infected the Israelites, God's chosen people.

So keeping, or the celebrating Easter in any manner, is an abomination to God, especially when it involves perverted practices to do with sex like Easter eggs and bunny rabbits, and services linked to ancient forms of Sun worship.

Easter should not be observed, practiced, or kept in any way by true Christians.

Halloween, or Hallowe'en, Spirits, Witchcraft, Ghoulies and Ghosties

According to the Etymological dictionary, 'Halloween' is a Scottish shortening of 'Allhallow-even' Eve of All Saints, last night of October" (1550s), the last night of the year in the old Celtic calendar, where it was Old Year's Night, a night for witches.

At Halloween, millions of parents encourage their children to dress up in weird costumes, and threaten neighbours with playing nasty 'tricks' on them if they do not give them sweets or other gifts.

These children, dressed in ghoulish, horrid, demonic witch costumes, are encouraged by parents to go from door to door threatening to 'trick or treat' people in a demeaning and unworthy practice which could not be further removed from the practice of true Christianity. Fun? Not funny at all. Disgusting!

What on earth can any of this have to do with Christianity?? Nothing at all!

The practice of Hallowe'en reflects and is based on the fear of and worship of wicked spirits which no Christian should ever be involved in.

The Bible does not mention Halloween as such. However, both the ancient origins of Halloween and its modern customs show it to be a celebration based on false beliefs about the dead and invisible spirits, or demons.

Tens of millions of Halloween pumpkins, or 'jack-o'-lanterns' are sacrificed to evil spirits annually when they could have provided food for the hungry. Anciently, people asked for food in return for a prayer for the dead, and they would carry hollowed-out lanterns, with a candle inside representing the false notion that a soul was trapped in purgatory.

None of the beliefs behind hallowe'en, the immortality of the soul, purgatory, and prayers for the dead are based on the Bible. The dead are dead and know not anything.

Ecclesiastes 9:5 For the living know that they shall die: but the dead know not any thing, neither have they any more a reward;

People would not dream of burning their children, but they are quite happy to encourage them to dress up and play at being 'witches' and 'wizards', and demand money by menaces, which everyone knows is actually a crime.

Deuteronomy 18:10 There shall not be found among you any one that maketh his son or his daughter to pass through the fire, or that useth divination, or an observer of times, or an enchanter, or a witch.

Parents who claim to be 'Christian' should regard the whole business of Halloween with horror, and keep their children indoors.

1 Corinthians 10:19 What say I then? that the idol is any thing, or that which is offered in sacrifice to idols is any thing? 20 But I say, that the things which the Gentiles sacrifice, they sacrifice to devils, and not to God: and I would not that ye should have fellowship with devils. 21 Ye cannot drink the cup of the Lord, and the cup of devils: ye cannot be partakers of the Lord's table, and of the table of devils. 22 Do we provoke the Lord to jealousy? are we stronger than he?

Ancient Celts wore ghoulish costumes to appease wandering spirits, and offered sweets to the spirits to appease them. The Bible, on the other hand, does not permit merging false religious practices with the worship of God.

2 Corinthians 6:15 And what concord hath Christ with Belial? or what part hath he that believeth with an infidel? 16 And what agreement hath the temple of God with idols? for ye are the temple of the living God; as God hath said, I will dwell in them, and walk in them; and I will be their God, and they shall be my people. 17 Wherefore come out from among them, and be ye separate, saith the Lord, and touch not the unclean thing; and I will receive you. 18 And will be a Father unto you, and ye shall be my sons and daughters, saith the Lord Almighty.

The true Christian is clearly commanded to come away from and be separate from the pagan activities of worldly people.

Ghosts, vampires, werewolves, witches, and zombies mimicked during Hallowe'en are associated with the evil spirit world. The Bible clearly states many times that we should resist wicked spirit forces, not celebrate with them. We need the special help from God to resist evil entities, which are as real today as they were in Christ's time.

Ephesians 6:11 Put on the whole armour of God, that ye may be able to stand against the wiles of the devil. 12 For we wrestle not against flesh and blood, but against principalities, against powers, against the rulers of the darkness of this world, against spiritual wickedness in high places. 3

Wherefore take unto you the whole armour of God, that ye may be able to withstand in the evil day, and having done all, to stand.

When we pray, we daily ask 'deliver us from evil' (or the evil ones). We need that protection.

Jeremiah 1:16 And I will utter my judgments against them touching all their wickedness, who have forsaken me, and have burned incense unto other gods, and worshipped the works of their own hands.

It is tragic that the congregations of 'Churchianity' do not realise what they are doing when they allow themselves to engage in Hallowe'en! Or when they fill their churches with all the images, likenesses, pictures, relics, etc., which God absolutely forbids.

Astrology

Astrology is a human system using Astronomical information in a perverted way. It suggests that the position of the heavenly bodies, the planets and the stars, somehow influences the birth, the personality, and the life that a person leads. This in a way, is 'worshipping' the heavens, rather than looking to God for guidance.

Every newspaper or magazine has their section on the 'Stars'. The gullible public, and around 25% of churchgoers pay more attention to what they say than they do to what God has to say about this subject. They actually give more credence to what journalistic astrologers write about their 'birth sign'. A quick comparison of these 'prophecies' will reveal what nonsense they are.

Astrologers are false prophets that make predictions that rarely if ever come to pass. Can all people born at a certain time and section in the Zodiac possibly be subject to the same notions? Hardly.

Jeremiah 10:2 Thus saith the Lord, Learn not the way of the heathen, and be not dismayed at the signs of heaven; for the heathen are dismayed at them.

Anything that we do, think, or read about that takes our minds away from God and His Word is not something a true Christian will want to be involved with.

What about homosexuality? Same sex marriages? Now referred to as 'LGBTQI'?

What follows on this subject are not the words of this author, but the Words of God Almighty which should be heeded by one and all.

Once homosexuality was known by the vast majority of people and Christians in particular to be wrong, but these practices in any form are now accepted almost as the norm.

Leviticus 18:22 Thou shalt not lie with mankind, as with womankind: it is abomination.

If God says it is an abomination, who are we to argue? Now openly homosexual church ministers, male and female, and members of Church congregations boldly claim to be Christians, and protest their right to live as they choose, in defiance of the clear laws of God on any aspect of LGBTQI. Often they make their declarations in the name of 'human rights', but human beings have no 'rights' when it comes to the matter of defying God's Law.

Deuteronomy 22:5 The woman shall not wear that which pertaineth unto a man, neither shall a man put on a woman's garment: for all that do so are abomination unto the Lord thy God.

Transvestitism is also to be deplored, not exploited.

Bi-sexuality is a tendency to be discouraged, not investigated or practiced.

There are millions who claim 'human rights' but in truth, under God, and in His presence, we have no 'rights' as humans. We rely, whether we realise it or not, upon God for every breath, and every heartbeat we are given.

Leviticus 18:23 Neither shalt thou lie with any beast to defile thyself therewith: neither shall any woman stand before a beast to lie down thereto: it is confusion.

Bestiality is an activity that should never enter into anyone's mind.

Paul makes this abundantly clear in the very first chapter of Romans.

Romans 1:26 For this cause God gave them up unto vile affections: for even their women did change the natural use into that which is against nature: 27 And likewise also the men, leaving the natural use of the woman, burned in their lust one toward another; men with men working that which is unseemly, and receiving in themselves that recompence of their error which was meet (HIV? AIDS? STD's?) 28 And even as they did not like to retain God in their knowledge, God gave them over to a reprobate mind, to do those things which are not convenient;

The whole matter of sex is sacred to God and should be respected as such.

Genesis 2:23 And Adam said, This is now bone of my bones, and flesh of my flesh: she shall be called Woman, because she was taken out of Man. 24 Therefore shall a man leave his father and his mother, and shall cleave unto his wife: and they shall be one flesh. 25 And they were both naked, the man and his wife, and were not ashamed.

The matrimonial bed is sacrosanct, pure, and Holy, and a wonderful gift to us.

Hebrews 13:4 Marriage is honourable in all, and the bed undefiled: but whoremongers and adulterers God will judge.

The goal of all Christians is the Kingdom of God
Matthew 6:33 But seek ye first the kingdom of God, and his righteousness; and all these things shall be added unto you.

We need to understand that nobody who practices any of these immoral acts will be candidates for the Kingdom of God.

1 Corinthians 6:9 Know ye not that the unrighteous shall not inherit the kingdom of God? Be not deceived: neither fornicators, nor idolaters, nor adulterers, nor effeminate, nor abusers of themselves with mankind, 10 Nor thieves, nor covetous, nor drunkards, nor revilers, nor extortioners, shall inherit the kingdom of God.

One can only hope and pray that God will show them what they are missing by defying Him.

Isaiah 3:9 The shew of their countenance doth witness against them; and they declare their sin as Sodom, they hide it not. Woe unto their soul! for they have rewarded evil unto themselves.

Could this be referring to those who flaunt their defiance to God in 'gay pride' or other types of parade?

CONCLUSION: The many practices of 'Churchianity' are not Christian.
Isaiah 1:14 Your new moons and your appointed feasts my soul hateth: they are a trouble unto me; I am weary to bear them.

God says very plainly in His Word, he hates these activities, so true Christians will not do or be involved with any of these things.

These ancient festivals were the basis of much folklore, and led to the weird customs practiced each year by religious and secular people alike in 'Christian' countries.

Now 'Christians' who become aware of the real meaning of Christmas, Lent, Easter, Halloween, Astrology, Homosexuality, (LGBTQI), same-sex marriages, racially mixed marriages, and what is behind all these practices, will need to have a huge change of attitude.

Also worshipping wealth, coveting possessions, chariots (cars!), and any form of sexual deviant behaviour, and the 'Christian' lands where churches are full of idols, all these are things which God hates.

Isaiah 2:7 Their land also is full of silver and gold, neither is there any end of their treasures; their land is also full of horses, neither is there any end of their chariots:

None of the unholy activities described in this chapter have anything to do with being a Christian; you cannot practice any of them, and be a true follower of Christ.

We do not need those who call themselves 'Apostles', Ministers, Prophets or any man to teach us.
No form of Christianity should be used as a form of control. Christianity was never intended to be used to exert any form of control over others, or dictate to others what they should or should not do.

Matthew 20:25 But Jesus called them unto him, and said, Ye know that the princes of the Gentiles exercise dominion over them, and they that are great exercise authority upon them. 26 But it shall not be so among you: but whosoever will be great among you, let him be your minister (Greek diakonos a servant); 27 And whosoever will be chief among you, let him be your servant (Greek doulos or slave):

Christ's words make it really clear, that we do not have dominion over other people. In Genesis, God gave man dominion over the fauna and flora, but it does not mention that He gave dominion over other humans.

1 Peter 5:3 Neither as being lords over God's heritage, but being examples to the flock.

No person in any organisation of men, regardless of their title or position, has any God-given authority over others.

It is this controlling aspect of the thousands of different church denominations of this world that completely misuse Christ's life, His teachings, His death and His resurrection. They use their interpretation of 'Christian' as a means of subjugating and controlling their followers which was never intended by God or Christ Jesus. In all human forms of 'Christianity', and every organisation of humans, have the desire to control at their roots.

Men and women group together into denominations, and formulate their own version of the Gospel, their own choice of doctrines, and their own ideas of which views they wish to enforce on their adherents. This is the opposite of submitting themselves to God, and teaching all they claim to lead to submit themselves to the Law of Love, and the direction of the Holy Spirit brought by Christ Jesus. Christians all need to submit to the rule of Christ Jesus in their minds and hearts.

We do not need any Apostles, any Ministers, any Prophets, Evangelists, or any man to teach us how to be saved, or teach us any other doctrines of Christianity. Why not? Because Christ tells us through His brother John, that it is God's Power transmitted by the flow of the Holy Spirit through our mind that will transmit Christ's teaching to us and help us grow.

*1 John 2:27 But the anointing which ye have received of him abideth in you, and **ye need not that any man teach you**: but as the same anointing teacheth you of all things, and is truth, and is no lie, and even as it hath taught you, ye shall abide in him.*

We have the man Jesus Christ teaching us by means of God's Holy Spirit, **and He is the one and only mediator** between God the Father and man, and we need none other. We certainly do not need any man, or any organisation of human beings to tell us what we have to do to be true Christians. God has given us all the information we need in His Word, and through the flow of Holy Spirit as we study and commune with God.

*1 Timothy 2:4 Who will have all men to be saved, and to come unto the knowledge of the truth. 5 **For there is one God, and one mediator between God and men, the man Christ Jesus;** 6 Who gave himself a ransom for all, to be testified in due time.*

'Churchianity' does not believe this Scripture. If they really did believe that this was indeed the Word of God speaking to us today, they would resign immediately their ecclesiastical positions. (from Greek ekklesiastikos " in late Greek, "of the church," from ekklesiastes "speaker in an assembly or church, preacher,").

Ignoring that clear statement in God's Word, ministers of man-made religions, mere humans, take it upon themselves to mediate for their followers and parishioners between God and them. Even to the extent of 'forgiving sin' and meting out punishments for what they consider sin. HORRORS! They can do no such thing, they have no authority to do so, and that is a fraudulent and dishonest claim, and it denies Christ's Sacrifice and His Authority.

We do not need any man, as we already through Christ, have free access to the Father, and even are allowed to call Him 'Abba' or 'Dad'!

*Galatians 4:6 And because ye are sons, God hath sent forth the Spirit of his Son into your hearts, crying, **Abba**, Father.*

Christ is the Firstborn. Because we are **'in'** Christ, part of His very 'body' the ecclesia, we are Firstborn children of God, and that is a wonderful thing to have learned from His Word. However, nobody can learn that if they do not have total confidence that the Holy Bible is God talking to us directly.

In our 21st century world, people are still coming up with weird and strange notions concerning the truths of the Bible, exactly as Paul, Peter, John and others warned about centuries ago.

1 Timothy 4:1 Now the Spirit speaketh expressly, that in the latter times some shall depart from the faith, giving heed to seducing spirits, and doctrines of devils;

Claiming to be a mediator between God and their parishioners is a false doctrine and directly opposite to God's wishes.

2 Peter 3:3 Knowing this first, that there shall come in the last days scoffers, walking after their own lusts,

The 'lust' of having their own way when they trample God's gift of pure sex into the mire in the vanity of their own carnal minds.

Galatians 1:6 I marvel that ye are so soon removed from him that called you into the grace of Christ unto another gospel: 7 Which is not another; but there be some that trouble you, and would pervert the gospel of Christ.

Adam and Eve had the opportunity to eat of the 'Tree of Life' and gain eternal life. But instead, Eve chose to listen to the serpent, disobey God, and eat of the 'Tree of the Knowledge of Good & Evil', and give some to Adam.

At which moment the Holy Spirit was take from Adam and Eve, and they immediately died spiritually, and they were thrown out of the Garden of Eden, and prevented from returning, making it impossible to eat of the 'Tree of Life'.

Genesis 3:22 And the LORD God said, Behold, the man is become as one of us, to know good and evil: and now, lest he put forth his hand, and take also of the tree of life, and eat, and live for ever: 23 Therefore the LORD God sent him forth from the garden of Eden, to till the ground from whence he was taken. 24 So he drove out the man; and he placed at the east of the garden of Eden Cherubims, and a flaming sword which turned every way, to keep the way of the tree of life.

When the First Adam was created, he had the Holy Spirit. When the Second Adam came, He also had the Holy Spirit from conception. The embryo of Jesus Christ was not made from Joseph's sperm or Mary's ovum, and she did not produce the baby in her womb. God the Father created that embryo that became Christ Jesus from the Spirit Essence of the Word into flesh, and placed it into her body.

John 1:1 In the beginning was the Word, and the Word was with God, and the Word was God. Then verse 14 And the Word was made flesh, and dwelt among us, (and we beheld his glory, the glory as of the only begotten of the Father,) full of grace and truth.

So the Word became flesh, and that flesh was not wicked in any way, it was Holy. Christ said in John 6:-

John 6:53 Then Jesus said unto them, Verily, verily, I say unto you, Except ye eat the flesh of the Son of man, and drink *his blood, ye have no life in you. 54 **Whoso eateth my flesh, and drinketh my blood, hath eternal life; and I will raise him up at the last day.** 55 For my flesh is meat indeed, and my blood is drink indeed. 56 He that eateth my flesh, and drinketh my blood, dwelleth in me, and I in him. 57 As the living Father hath sent me, and I live by the Father: so he that eateth me, even he shall live by me.*

Since Christ's death, there is no need for any Christian to observe the Lord's Supper, or Eucharist. All physical rituals have been replaced by Spiritual concepts of the new law.

It is important to understand that this in John 6 is all figurative, symbolic language. The Catholic Church purists claim that the bread and the wine of the Eucharist are actually transformed into the actual flesh and blood of Christ as the recipient takes them. This, the Catholic Hierarchy say is an article of faith. They are not willing to consider that the words of Christ are figurative and symbolic.

Eating the flesh and blood of a human being is clearly against the Old Testament law, and although Christ brought the New Covenant Law of Love, all physical aspects of the Old Law were superseded by the Spiritual. For example Circumcision and the sacrificial system. But cannabalism would still be against God's Law of Love!

So we fleshly mortals will put on immortality. When? At the last day, which for those of us who are alive, will be at Christ's return at the resurrection of the dead. It does not mean that we have that life right now, because we have not yet taken of the 'Tree of Life' yet. Although *in type* we have, we have in a nascent sense, but we have not experienced it yet in a physical way, and will not until the resurrection of the dead at Christ's coming at the end of the age.

In the book of Revelation, it talks of 'Trees of Life' which bear fruit monthly so that people, men and women who qualify in the Millennium, and afterwards, will be able to eat of that fruit and gain healing and eternal life.

Revelation 22:2 In the midst of the street of it, and on either side of the river, was there the tree of life, which bare twelve manner of fruits, and yielded her fruit every month: and the leaves of the tree were for the healing of the nations.

We who are true Christians now, redeemed by the blood of Christ, will not need to eat of those trees, as we will already have been given the gift of eternal life, and will be immortal eternally living Spirit Beings, part of the Family of God, even when God the Father is on Earth.

All this shows is that human beings do not have immortality in any form right now. The human spirit is loaned to each of us by God which He takes back at death. It is God's gift of the human spirit that enlivens us and gives us 'mind', it does not belong to us.

Everything we are and have, breath, life itself, all are gifts from God.
We do not have any life of ourselves, as a feotus we rely on the life of the mother to grow and develop. As we are born, we have our own 'life' which God puts into us at birth with our first breath, and takes back at death.

Every breath, every gift that we have, every factor of Salvation, every concept or moral ideas we embrace in our minds, the teachings of the Bible, belief, knowledge, faith, repentance, and that we can confess Christ from the heart; ALL of that and more has been given to us by God to work with in this *life* which itself is also a gift from God. We do not have life inherently, only God does.

It is not what *we* have to do on our own that gets us saved, the work we do will earn us rewards, but will not get us saved. The fact that we believe in Christ at all is a gift to us personally from God.

'Christian' ministers are fond of quoting a verse (out of its own context) which tells us to 'work out our own salvation', but they do not read and emphasise the following verse which is part of the complete thought.

Philippians 2:12 Wherefore, my beloved, as ye have always obeyed, not as in my presence only, but now much more in my absence, work out your own salvation with fear and trembling.

Yes, as Christians we do have to work, but we do not have to work out our salvation as we are already saved. The works we do have to do are spiritual and physical things in accordance with God's New Covenant laws in order to qualify for entrance into the Kingdom of God. However, these works will enable us to receive a position commensurate with our work, but it is God and Christ who have actually already done all the work needed to grant us Salvation.

*Philippians 2:13 For it is **God** which worketh in you both to will and to do of his good pleasure.*

God's only begotten Son was willing to give up His position in the Father and Son Family Godhead to become human and die for us.

John 6:38 For I came down from heaven, not to do mine own will, but the will of him that sent me.

We do _not_ go to heaven when we die as so many are taught to believe.

John 3:13 And no man hath ascended up to heaven, but he that came down from heaven, even the Son of man which is in heaven.

That was true when Christ said it, and is still true today. Again, we need to trust and believe the Bible which contains the clear evidence is that we do not have life inherently, only God does.

Human beings are born to live and to ***die, dead!*** Not to live on in some form of ethereal existence.

Every person who has ever lived has sinned.

Romans 3:23 For all have sinned, and come short of the glory of God;

*Ezekiel 18:4 Behold, all souls are mine; as the soul of the father, so also the soul of the son is mine: **the soul that sinneth, it shall die.***

This is another clear example in God's Word of repetition for emphasis.

Ezekiel 18:20a Yet say ye, Why? doth not the son bear the iniquity of the father? When the son hath done that which is lawful and right, and hath kept all my statutes, and hath done them, he shall surely live. 20 **The soul that sinneth, it shall die...**

Here is another example of 'progressive revelation', where the old law in *Exodus 20:5 'visiting the iniquity of the fathers upon the children unto the third and fourth generation of them that hate me'* is rescinded under Christ's inspiration, and no longer applies.

Ezekiel 18:20b The son shall not bear the iniquity of the father, neither shall the father bear the iniquity of the son:

the righteousness of the righteous shall be upon him, and the wickedness of the wicked shall be upon him.

However the penalty for sin is still death for the individual for their own sin. As we know, that penalty has already been paid for us by Christ's sacrifice.

Romans 6:23 For the wages of sin is death; but the gift of God is eternal life through Jesus Christ our Lord.

Yes, but the glorious truth of the Gospel is that we will be raised from the dead at the resurrection, or if we are alive, we shall be changed from flesh into Spirit and live together with Christ Jesus for eternity. We can thank God for that amazing future that awaits us.

So if nobody goes to heaven when they die, what does happen?

NEITHER DOES ANYONE GO TO AN EVER-BURNING HELL

This concept was introduced as part of the desire of churches to control their adherents with fear. Much of this false teaching is based on Dante's poem 'The Divine Comedy'. Supposed to describe three aspects of a Christian live, it was absorbed into Christian churches in the Middle Ages around 1200 A.D. The parts on the Inferno and Purgatory pictured the torment and cleansing process a Christian had to go through after death. This was complete fantasy, with no truth in it at all. Yes the belief in Hell-fire is prominent in the minds of billions all over the world.

Misunderstandings of the subject of fire in the Bible are also promulgated in such a manner as to instil unreasonable fear in people.

WHEN WE DIE, WE ARE DEAD, NO CONSCIOUSNESS, NOTHING

We are corruptible, Greek *phthartos* – perishable, corruptible, when God takes back our spirit, our dead bodies decay and rot away. From dust we have come and to dust we shall return.

Dust + human spirit + breath of life = Living Soul

Living Soul – human spirit – breath of life = Dead body becomes dust.

*Ecclesiastes 9:5 For the living know that they shall **die: but the dead know not any thing**, neither have they any more a reward; for the memory of them is forgotten. 6 Also their love, and their hatred, and their envy, (all memory, feeling and emotion) is now perished; neither have they any more a portion (no involvement at all) for ever in any thing that is done under the sun.*

*Ecclesiastes 9:10 Whatsoever thy hand findeth to do, do it with thy might; **for there is no work, nor device, nor knowledge, nor wisdom, in the grave**, whither thou goest.*

The twelfth chapter of Ecclesiastes describes the process of getting old and dying in a very picturesque, beautiful and poetic way. Verse 1 speaks of the time when we are aged, and we no longer have pleasure in living each day. Verse 2 talks about the sun, moon, and stars being 'darkened' as eyesight fails. Verse 3 tells of the time when the 'keepers of the house', the legs will tremble; and the 'grinders are few' as we lose our teeth.

Verse 4 refers to sleep being disturbed even with quiet sounds like birds singing. Verse 5 And the time comes when the old are afraid of heights, afraid of falling over; when our muscles lose their strength, so weak that a grasshopper would be a burden; desire will diminish and fail; because we are on our way to our 'long home', the grave, and people who mourn us are in the streets.

Verse 6 tells of the 'silver cord', the symbol of our spiritual connection with God is 'loosed'; and the 'golden bowl', the water 'pitcher', and the 'wheel' are broken. These last three symbols may well be talking about the heart and circulation ceasing to function.

Then verse 7 says 'Then shall the dust return to the earth as it was' as we decay in the grave; **and the (human) spirit shall return to God who gave it to us.**

But remember the illustration of the two identical Bibles. If we put our trust in the Bible 'on the left' and give any credence at all to the serpent's words, *'you shall not die'*, every verse that speaks about death from then on to the last page of the Bible will be interpreted differently as not really meaning what it says.

It is crucial for all who would aspire to be true Christians to ask continuously for the gifts of belief, faith and trust in the purity, accuracy and truth of the Scriptures of the Holy Bible.

So many people only have a weak belief about whether the Bible is actually the Word of God, they harbour doubts. They hear so many times that the Bible is full of error, and its being discredited in so many ways, neither of which is true. This leads them to decide they will 'cherry pick' the scriptures, and only believe what they are told it says by religious 'authorities', or what they think it means, or what they want to believe it says. This is the pathway to total confusion.

1 Corinthians 14:33 For God is not the author of confusion, but of peace, as in all ~~churches~~ *ecclesia of the saints.*

To be a Christian, in Dr. Martin's illustration, we have to believe and trust the Bible 'on the right' and take God's Word for it that when we die we truly are dead. From then on from Genesis to Revelation every scripture that is about life and death will give us more of the truth.

So what does happen after death?
Our amazing, breathtaking, glorious future is far away and beyond our wildest dreams or our imagination. It is so much more than just going to heaven when you die only to strum on a harp as some think. An exciting glimpse of our time with God after our resurrection is covered in chapter seven.

The Worldwide Rebellion against Authority
Satan, the Adversary, under God the Father, is the ruler of this world and is deceiving as many of the world's population as he can. Few in 'Churchianity' understand from the Scriptures that God through Christ created Satan, who is doing what he does, because that was what he was created to do. As hard as this might be to grasp, our God of Love chose this way in order to bring His human Children to Glory. If there had been a better way to do it, God would have done it a different way.

Revelation 12:9 And the great dragon was cast out, that old serpent, called the Devil, and Satan, which deceiveth the whole world: he was cast out into the earth, and his angels were cast out with him.

There is an almost universal worldwide movement, especially now in these latter times, for people to choose to believe what others tell them to believe, or what they choose to think is true, rather than accept the authority of God's Word. In fact this refusal to accept responsibility has become the way of life for most of the human race. God rejection is the way of life for most. It wasn't my fault… I thought…

Satan wants to foment the attitude of rebellion against all forms of authority, and especially against the Authority of God Almighty. The entire Bible is the sad story of human beings rebelling against God and His Loving Rule of Law.

This rebelliousness is what is at the root of the Bible reading population of this Earth. For the most part, they are people who decide that they will choose their own beliefs out of the Bible regardless of what God says. The people who call themselves 'Christian', in too many cases pick and choose what they will believe, and in the process reject the fundamental bases of Christianity.

Few children are taught to respect and obey the authority of their parents any more. Schoolteachers despair at the rebellious attitude and disrespectful behaviour in schools which began at home. Young children and adults of all ages who rebel against the laws of the land and of society now fill our young offender's areas, and fill prisons over their capacity, and cause the need for more to be built.

THIS PRESENT EVIL WORLD – IS FILLED WITH SATANIC BELIEFS

Satan encourages people to dabble with the spirit world and they do.

World leaders in positions of power realise that 'power corrupts, and that absolute power corrupts absolutely'. Unfortunately, few if any rulers appear to be aware of the extent to which they are influenced by unseen corrupt spirit entities. Make no mistake, these entities may not be visible, but they are most certainly real.

Many use their power without restraint to control those they reign over. It is not difficult to observe what goes on in this world, and appreciate that wicked spirits are undoubtedly involved with many of the inhumane atrocities that go on.

Ephesians 6:12 For we wrestle not against flesh and blood, but against principalities, against powers, against the rulers of the darkness of this world, against spiritual wickedness in high places.

Realising this, Christians need to pray to be able to live a quiet and peaceful life, and are encouraged to obey the laws of those who rule over us. And to pray for those who do rule over us, even if we find it difficult to like them, it is our responsibility to respect them, and pray for them.

1 Timothy 2:1 I exhort therefore, that, first of all, supplications, prayers, intercessions, and giving of thanks, be made for all men; 2 For kings, and for all that are in authority; that we may lead a quiet and peaceable life in all godliness and honesty. 3 For this is good and acceptable in the sight of God our Saviour;

True Christians also need to be aware that spirit entities abound in this world, and their aim is to interfere with the plan of God, and harass, confuse and impede His children in their search for Godliness.

Even in some 'Christian' churches, getting in touch with spirits, going into trance mode, speaking in tongues, and other satanic practices are even encouraged as part of their services of worship.

The large number of programmes featured on television and in all forms of the modern media, present titillating titbits of information supposedly gleaned from the spirit world and from those who have 'passed over to the other side'. This presupposes that those persons who have died are living somewhere with some form of consciousness, and are able in the right circumstances, to communicate with people who are alive on this earth. This simply is not true according to the plain statements regarding death in the Bible.

Wicked 'spirits' can, and they most certainly do communicate with humans. In fact it happens whenever they are able or allowed by weak people to do it. Those people who engage in any type of activity with 'mediums' are playing with fire. They have no idea what they are dealing with.

Think of all the horrors in the world, the ghastly war toll, the horrendous practice of torture, 'ethnic cleansing', the genital mutilation of young girls, the cruelty of Sharia Law, man's inhumanity to man, rebellion against the laws of sex laid down by our Creator, and so on. They are not human activities. Rebellious spirits are involved with all these things, encouraging human beings to be inhumane, cruel and demonic.

Christ Jesus told us to pray daily for God to deliver us from evil, or from the evil ones. To use contact with spirit powers as a form of entertainment is just another symptom of the rebelliousness of the world against the Law of Love.

1 Timothy 4:1 Now the Spirit speaketh expressly, that in the latter times some shall depart from the faith, giving heed to seducing spirits, and doctrines of devils;

People in some 'Churchianity' organisations seem more interested in finding out more about the relationship between spirits and human beings (which they should not!), when they should be learning more about the relationship between human beings and their Spiritual Father and Brother Christ Jesus. It seems many want to enter into discussions on topics which run counter to the Scriptures which should be left severely alone and avoided at all cost.

There are other types of spirit beings abroad in the world

2 Corinthians 11:3 But I fear, lest by any means, as the serpent beguiled Eve through his subtlety, so your minds should be corrupted from the simplicity that is in Christ.

What is Paul talking about here? It is a corrupted gospel. He is talking about the lie the serpent told Eve about the Immortality of the Soul, and the lie that part of us does not die, and that people die but go to heaven! Paul calls this 'another gospel' when people entertain ideas that come from a different spirit which might sound like the Christian Gospel, but it is as far from the Truth as East is from West.

*2 Corinthians 11:4 For if he that cometh preacheth another Jesus, whom we have not preached, or if ye receive **another spirit**, which ye have not received, or another gospel, which ye have not accepted, ye might well bear with him.*

Ministers of some churches look and sound so very good as they expound on human relationships, loving others, and so on, but inwardly are ravening wolves. Without their audience having any idea, they are teaching the Bible in such a manner that will lead their hearers slowly but surely away from the truths of Christianity.

Matthew 7:14 Beware of false prophets, which come to you in sheep's clothing, but inwardly they are ravening wolves.

This is not the author of this book speaking; it is our Lord and Saviour, the Creator of all things speaking to us today. He says:

The ministers of this world's churches are not at all what they appear to be.

2 Corinthians 11:13 For such are false apostles, deceitful workers, transforming themselves into the apostles of Christ. 14 And no marvel; for Satan himself is transformed into an angel of light. 15 Therefore it is no great thing if his ministers also be transformed as the ministers of righteousness; whose end shall be according to their works.

Such religious leaders talk about 'love', and that the 'spirit' is moving, and everything they say is so very appealing to those who are deceived.

Speaking in tongues.
Some charismatic groups arouse and work up the 'spirit' and have people moved by the 'spirit' speaking in 'tongues', but they are probably unaware that the 'spirit' they are talking about is definitely NOT the Holy Spirit. The Holy Spirit does not speak. Nor is the Holy Spirit the third person in the Godhead as is suggested by the false doctrine of the 'Trinity' as was mentioned earlier.

John 16:13 Howbeit when he (it), the Spirit of truth, is come, he (it) will guide you into all truth: for he (actually 'it' – God's Power) **shall not speak of himself***; but whatsoever he (it) shall hear, that shall he (it) speak (not in words, but in terms of thoughts, ideas, and concepts) and he (it, God's Power) will shew you things to come.*

When anyone in the Bible spoke in tongues, everyone in the audience heard what was being said ***in their own language***.

Acts 2:4 And they were all filled with the Holy Ghost, and began to speak with other tongues, as the Spirit gave them utterance. 5 And there were dwelling at Jerusalem Jews, devout men, out of every nation under heaven. 6 Now when this was noised abroad, the multitude came together, and were confounded, because that every man heard them speak in his own language. 7 And they were all amazed and marvelled, saying one to another, Behold, are not all these which speak Galilaeans? 8 And how hear we every man in our own tongue, wherein we were born? 9 Parthians, and Medes, and Elamites, and the dwellers in Mesopotamia, and in Judaea, and Cappadocia, in Pontus, and Asia, 10 Phrygia, and Pamphylia, in Egypt, and in the parts of Libya about Cyrene, and strangers of Rome, Jews and proselytes, 11 Cretes and Arabians, we do hear them speak in our tongues the wonderful works of God.

The speaking in tongues was not some unintelligible babble, that needed someone to interpret what the 'spirit' was saying, that is featured in some denominations. Those in the crowd from all those countries listed in Acts heard what was being said in their native tongue, the language of the country where they were born.

1 Corinthians 12:9 To another faith by the same Spirit; to another the gifts of healing by the same Spirit; 10 To another the working of miracles; to another prophecy; to another discerning of spirits; to another divers kinds of tongues; to another the interpretation of tongues:

This is talking about some having the gift of speaking several languages, French, Spanish, German, etc., others have the gift of being able to translate from one language to another language.

This is not talking about meaningless babble that nobody except the 'interpreter' can understand, it is simply talking about the gift of tongues which means languages.

This is talking about a person speaking clearly in one language, who has an interpreter to put it into another language, so that one from a different country can understand what is being said.

*1 John 4:1 Beloved, believe not every spirit, but **try** the spirits whether they are of God: because many false prophets are gone out into the world.*

This word in Greek either *dokimazo* or *petrazo* translated 'try' mean to test, to scrutinize, to examine for truth, to prove authentic, to discern. Do not just accept what you hear and see, test it against the truth of God's Word.

Mediums and Psychics

People watch television and listen while a 'psychic' or 'medium' ask for questions from the audience about people that have died in their family. The questions are almost always about inconsequential and trivial matters. Like where did granddad hide his gold watch? Or whether they are happy where they are. The psychic perhaps goes into a type of trance, maybe their voice changes a great deal as the audience is told that the spirit of the dead person is speaking 'through' the medium.

Those attending the studio audiences of these shows are rapt with attention as they listen to the lies being told by the spirit the medium is 'channelling'. Many of these performers are genuinely psychic, individuals who may well be in touch with evil spirits, but many are charlatans who fool the public into thinking they are in touch with relatives when of course they are not.

We should not be the least bit interested in what 'spirits' have to say, but only what the Word of God has to tell us. We need to guard against giving any attention at all to those who are in touch with the 'spirit' world. We do not have to get any type of revelation from 'spirit' beings who are out to trick us.

If any person thought an angel had brought them a message, unless that 'message' resonated accurately with the Word of

God it should be rejected immediately, and cause them to offer up a prayer for protection from that evil spirit.

Dr. Martin once mentioned that for the last two years he was with the Foundation for Biblical Research (FBR), almost everyone in the office seemed to believe in the immortality of the soul. Some were even looking to 'prove' that notion from the Bible which of course is totally impossible to do, as the Bible all through its pages teaches that the dead are indeed dead. And that hostile attitude frankly was at the basis of the reasons his 'Christian' colleagues gave for his dismissal from the FBR, because Dr. Martin was adamant in his belief that when the Bible says *'dead'*, it means ***'dead'***!

Back in the Old Testament, King Saul contacted a witch because the Lord had not seemed to answer his prayers.

1 Samuel 28:3 Now Samuel was dead, and all Israel had lamented him, and buried him in Ramah, even in his own city. And Saul had put away those that had familiar spirits, and the wizards, out of the land.

Saul was a wicked king, but at least had gone some way to getting rid of those with 'familiar' or evil spirits. But now, he was frightened at the prospect of his nation being attacked and beaten by the Philistines. Saul approached God in the ways he knew, but received no response because God had withdrawn from Saul. So Saul decided to work things out his own way and contact a witch for information from her 'familiar spirit'.

1 Samuel 28:5 And when Saul saw the host of the Philistines, he was afraid, and his heart greatly trembled. 6 And when Saul enquired of the Lord, the Lord answered him not, neither by dreams, nor by Urim, nor by prophets. 7 Then said Saul unto his servants, Seek me a woman that hath a familiar spirit, that I may go to her, and enquire of her. And his servants said to him, Behold, there is a woman that hath a familiar spirit at Endor.

This 'witch' claimed to have brought up Samuel who was dead, and she claimed an apparition appeared and spoke to her. Saul talked with this 'person', but this was an 'evil spirit' masquerading as, or impersonating Samuel, and it told Saul that the Philistines would win the battle which they did.

Wicked spirits often speak the 'truth' or give some accurate information in order so much better to deceive those who believe that dead people are not dead, and to believe in what the 'spirit' says. This was the case in Acts 16 when a young girl possessed with an evil spirit followed Paul and Silas a round shouting day after day that 'These men are the servants of the most high God, which shew unto us the way of salvation.' What she (or actually the evil spirit) was saying was absolutely true. Paul turned to her (not to the spirit) and said in verse 18, I command thee in the name of Jesus Christ to come out of her.' And he (the spirit) came out the same hour.

Notice carefully that Paul called on the name of Jesus Christ to eject the spirit; Paul did not attempt to address the spirit by himself. Neither should we, we can do no better than follow Paul's example, and pray for God and Christ to deal with it.

Acts 19:13 Then certain of the vagabond Jews, exorcists, took upon them to call over them which had evil spirits the name of the Lord *Jesus, saying, We adjure you by Jesus whom Paul preacheth. 14 And there were seven sons of one Sceva, a Jew, and chief of the priests, which did so.*

Notice, seven men who practiced 'exorcism', claiming to get rid of spirits, took it upon themselves to call those over who had evil spirits, and said to them 'We adjure you by Jesus who Paul preacheth'. Big mistake.

Acts 19:15 And the evil spirit answered and said, Jesus I know, and Paul I know; but who are ye? 16 And the man in whom the evil spirit was leaped on them, and overcame them, and prevailed against them, so that they fled out of that house naked and wounded.

The spirit violently attacked them physically doing serious harm. This is a strong warning lesson recorded for our information here in the Bible not to mess with spirits or those who are possessed by them, or even attempt to deal with them!!

In this type of situation, call immediately for the support and pray for the help of Jesus Christ, address Him, Jesus Christ, do **NOT** address the person or the spirit, as you put yourself at risk if you do.

Also note in the case in Acts 16, there were serious repercussions from those who had been profiting financially from a 'medium's' activities.

Acts 16:16 And it came to pass, as we went to prayer, a certain damsel possessed with a spirit of divination met us, which brought her masters much gain by soothsaying: 17 The same followed Paul and us, and cried, saying, These men are the servants of the most high God, which shew unto us the way of salvation. 18 And this did she many days. But Paul, being grieved, turned and said to the spirit, I command thee in the name of Jesus Christ to come out of her. And he came out the same hour. 19 And when her masters saw that the hope of their gains was gone, they caught Paul and Silas, and drew them into the marketplace unto the rulers, 20 And brought them to the magistrates, saying, These men, being Jews, do exceedingly trouble our city, 21

And teach customs, which are not lawful for us to receive, neither to observe, being Romans. 22 And the multitude rose up together against them: and the magistrates rent off their clothes, and commanded to beat them. 23 And when they had laid many stripes upon them, they cast them into prison, charging the jailor to keep them safely:

There is a lot of money to be made by preying on people who believe that their dead relatives can be contacted. People who practice this and have their livelihood threatened are prone to attack anyone who might ruin their business, so be warned.

Embracing the idea that the dead are not dead, and having any involvement with the discussion whether or not it is possible to communicate with 'spirits' or they with us, is not only something a Christian should never be involved with, but is fraught with unrealised dangers. There are spirits out there, and they exist, they are a part of the truth of God which we should be alert for.

At the end of the age there are going to be people listening to 'spirits' and their teachings. We see this now on television and in séances through those who claim to be 'mediums'.

*1 Timothy 4:1 Now the Spirit speaketh expressly, that in the **latter** times some shall depart from the faith, giving heed to seducing spirits, and doctrines of devils;*

The fact is that in séances or in personal discussion with people who claim to be able to communicate with spirits, sometimes some truth emerges, or even positive 'miracles' happen. But this is no indication that this is an acceptable activity. It is not.

What the subject does not realise is that the 'spirit' is actually reading their mind, which is how the 'spirit' is able to tell the psychic things in their minds to repeat to the hapless client that nobody else in the world could know, thus convincing them that they are 'talking' to the dead relative.

We have to remember that our focus and our only contact with Spirit should be exclusively with God and His Son Christ Jesus either through reading His Word, or praying daily as we strive to grow in Grace and Knowledge.

In this connection, Dr. Martin told about his mother and father who died a few years ago. His mother died at just about ninety-one years of age. 'She and my father are buried up there in California in the central valley just a short distance from where I am speaking. It comforts me to know that they are there in that grave, and that they are dead. If I am still alive when Christ returns, we are all going to be resurrected at exactly the same time. Sometimes, he said, "I feel the same way Paul felt as he expressed in Philippians".

Philippians 1:23 For I am in a strait betwixt two, having a desire to depart, and to be with Christ; which is far better:

Once a person dies, consciousness ceases and we are dead as we read in Ecclesiastes 9:10. Four, forty, four hundred, or four thousand or more years may pass between death and the resurrection. But regardless of how much time elapses between our death and the resurrection, when we die, when we are next conscious, the very next moment, it will be just like awakening from sleep, we will be conscious and alive in the twinkling of an eye, and we will immediately be in the presence of Christ Jesus. Our future is a Spiritual one, and will be given to us by Christ Jesus at that time.

Dr. Martin also once explained: *'If some time in the future a spirit came to me saying things only my father or my mother would know, and even if either one appeared, most people would be deceived by that, and say, 'Oh there is my mother or father coming back from the dead to talk to me'. No way* *could that possibly be the case. I would instantly ask God in the name of Christ Jesus to get rid of that 'spirit', that evil influence from my sight and my mind. Because I would know that the whole thing was a **lie** from start to finish as my mother and my father are dead and buried. So if some spirit came impersonating my parents, which is exactly what it would be, I can tell them to leave immediately and I know without a question of any doubt that I will have Christ Jesus on my side helping me. I would pray in God's Holy name he would give me the protection you and I would need under those circumstances'.*

Good advice!

The use of pendulums.
Many people have different ways to contact the spirit world to get help with all kinds of decisions, and answers to questions they have that they do not think they can answer for themselves, some use tea leaves, or 'guided' writing, others may use a pendulum.

What happens in a session with a psychic is the same as with the pendulum. What the person swinging the pendulum does not realise is that the 'spirit' is reading *their* mind, and is influencing the physical matter of the pendulum to swing in a certain way. This is how the pendulum 'tells' the poor individual things nobody else in the world could know, which 'proves' to them that they are in touch with their dead wife, relative or friend, but of course they are not. It is all a lie and a hoax.

They attach a string to a crystal or some other object, and swing the crystal gently and watch for it to move in a certain way. Perhaps they will set up in their minds that if the crystal goes around in a circle it means 'yes', and if it just goes back and forth it means 'no'. Each person will choose their own 'code' whereby the crystal will indicate a yes/no answer to their question.

As a matter of interest, it is actually very difficult, almost impossible, to pose a question to which the answer is only 'yes' or 'no'. Involved with most questions are many other factors which would have to be take into account, so the answer 'yes' or 'no' is actually valueless.

THE 'ACID' TEST – WHO IS TALKING HERE?

*1 John 4:1 Beloved, believe not every spirit, but **try** the spirits whether they are of God: because many false prophets are gone out into the world.*

This word in Greek either *dokimazo* or *petrazo* translated 'try' mean to test, to scrutinize, to examine for truth, to prove authentic, to discern.

How do you 'test' or 'try' the spirits, or mediums, pendulums, or voices (even voices you recognise!), or apparitions, seances or any manifestation of anything that is, or is purported to be from someone who has died and we know are dead?

THE DEAD ARE <u>DEAD</u>, HAVE NO LIFE AT ALL, NO CONSCIOUSNESS, AND CANNOT SPEAK, SO WHO IS SPEAKING? EITHER THE SPIRIT OR SPIRITS ARE SPEAKING THROUGH THE PERSON, OR THE PERSON IS A FRAUD AND SPEAKING THEMSELVES.

So if there are any voices, or any other form of communication during one of these events, it is coming from what the Bible calls a 'familiar spirit', and dealing with them in any manner is forbidden by God.

*Leviticus 19:31 Regard not them that have **familiar spirits**, neither seek after wizards, to be defiled by them: I am the Lord your God.*

CONTACT ONLY GOD WHO IS A SPIRIT, OR JESUS CHRIST

On the other hand, in this age, when we ask for the help of the Holy Spirit as we study God's Word, we are doubtless going to see all kinds of the prophesied increase of knowledge spoken of by Daniel the Prophet. We are likely to learn new things of great import, and very exciting information from other sources like archaeology or useful books which will illuminate and expand our knowledge of the Bible.

And **we always have to check that what we are learning is absolutely in agreement with everything else the Bible and Christ's Word through the Holy Spirit has taught us.**

That is how we must 'test' and 'try' the 'spirit' of anything we hear or read, check it against what we *know* the Bible says on the subject.

A reminder, that if we do our part properly, diligently, prayerfully, we will not need any human to teach us. Again for emphasis and comfort:-

1 John 2:27 But the anointing which ye have received of him abideth in you, and ye need not that any man teach you: but as the same anointing teacheth you of all things, and is truth, and is no lie, and even as it hath taught you, ye shall abide in him.

The danger of "debating" doctrine with anyone without discernment

It is also very important to be willing to listen to others, but if they are attempting to 'debate' or 'argue' their case when it is clearly not congruent with the Holy Scriptures, then it is better to withdraw from the conversation.

Proverb 26:4 Answer not a fool according to his folly, lest thou also be like unto him. 5 Answer a fool according to his folly, lest he be wise in his own conceit.

This is not a contradiction! Discern whether to answer a 'fool' and make a fool of yourself, or not and still avoid debate, as it will probably lead to a worse situation.

2 Timothy 2:16 But shun profane and vain babblings: for they will increase unto more ungodliness.

Often people who believe in contacting the spirit world can be quite aggressive in their defence of their activities. If ever a Christian realises that a conversation might be becoming an argument or a debate, the wise thing is to exit from it immediately. 'Debating' is one of the fruits of the flesh, and should be avoided by Christians.

*Romans 1:29 Being filled with all unrighteousness, fornication, wickedness, covetousness, maliciousness; full of envy, murder, **debate**, deceit, malignity; whisperers,*

Strong's 2054) e]riv, — *er'-is*; of uncertain affinity; a *quarrel*, i.e. (by implication) *wrangling*: — contention, **debate**, strife, variance.

2 Corinthians 12:For I fear, lest, when I come, I shall not find you such as I would, and that I shall be found unto you such as ye would not: lest there be debates (Strong's 2054), envyings, wraths, strifes, backbitings, whisperings, swellings, tumults:

Stories about mediums and their activities are best avoided, no matter how interesting they might appear to be.

1 Timothy 1:4 Neither give heed to fables and endless genealogies, which minister questions, rather than godly edifying which is in faith: so do.

True Christians need to be cautious around those who are involved in 'Churchianity', and especially not be drawn into their activities, even if they are members of our family.

And if anyone should bring a point of the Bible to us, and if we see the need to learn from what they are saying, then we hope we will be willing to listen. We know we continually need to grow in grace and knowledge. That means we need to study to come to a clearer understanding of the Bible day by day, and year by year.

This whole chapter concerning "Churchianity' was not written to condemn or criticise anyone, merely to bring to those whose minds are open, God's will for us as Christians, some information that they may hitherto have not known or understood.

The quotes from the Bible may 'cut to the quick' for some people, but that is the nature of God's Word.

Hebrews 4:12 For the word of God is quick, and powerful, and sharper than any **twoedged sword**, piercing even to the dividing asunder of soul and spirit, and of the joints and marrow, and is a discerner of the thoughts and intents of the heart.

God's 'sword', His Word, gets right to the heart of things, to cut out those things which a person thinks about or does, which are keeping them from the contact with their Lord and Master Jesus Christ that they need.

CHAPTER 3

EVILUTION & SETI

THE THEORY & PURSUIT OF NONSENSE

Why 'EVILUTION'?
Because it denies the Creator God and proposes
that everything created itself, it is EVIL.
Why is SETI futile?

Because evidence of Intelligence is right here!

EVILUTION

Charles Robert Darwin, FRS., FRGS etc., was born on the 12th February 1809. He died 19th April 1882. He was an English naturalist, geologist, and biologist. He is best known for his contributions to the '**science**' of evolution.

The 'knowledge' Darwin had a hundred and eighty years ago as a 'Fellow of the Royal Society', and other such august bodies of peer scholars, compared to a young child in the 21st century, was not only rudimentary, ignorant of many things, but also hugely incorrect, and even ludicrous.

The expansion of knowledge in many branches of science shows this to be true. That does not stop people from believing the fables built on fables, or choosing to believe the theory of evolution, and other ludicrous ideas.

For many people, to criticise the 'Theory of Evolution' is like attacking a religion. In a sense it is, because to the 'true believer' in evolution, the whole concept is sacred. 'Evilution' is not sacred, it is sacrilegious! What does sacrilege mean?

Sacrilege *(n.) c. 1300, "crime of stealing what is consecrated to God," from Old French sacrilege (12c.), from Latin sacrilegium "temple robbery, a stealing of sacred things," from sacrilegus "stealer of sacred things," noun use of adjective, from phrase sacrum legere "to steal sacred things,*

To deny that God Is, and to deny and refute that God Created all things, and to give all the 'credit' to the 'created' for forming itself, is sacrilege, that is stealing from God! Not only that, it is both rude and insulting to the Creator God.

Imagine of you will, if when looking at some of the finest furniture ever made like Chippendale; the finest musical instruments in the world like a Steinway & Sons grand piano, a Stradivarius violin; and you suggested that they were made by some amateur in a back street. Not only would that be ridiculous, but also insulting to the makers.

In the same way, when we observe the complexity of the DNA molecule, the incredible intricacy of the food chain on earth, the enormity of the Universe and the accuracy of its 'clock', and the unexplained wonder of 'life' itself; then consider that some 'scientists' insist that all this, and all we know of and experience came about, developed and 'evolved' itself from 'nothing' as a result of a 'Big Bang'.

If that is not a calculated insult to the Maker, what is? It is also willing ignorance of the most profound degree.

Some religious people straddle the fence, (always a most uncomfortable position!) and have devised a compromise. They call it 'Theistic Evolution', which suggests that God created all things by the method suggested by evolutionists. He did not.

CHRISTIANITY DIRECT FROM CHRIST – THE WORD OF GOD

That is, that everything God created in one form, which then adapted and redesigned itself over millions or billions of years. By doing so, they make a 'god' (small 'g') to worship out of 'the theory' and out of 'science' falsely so-called, and all physical matter.

The real God does not appreciate that, and thunders,

"Thou shalt have no other gods before me".

Is the 'Theory of Evolution' scientific?

The meaning of the word 'science' is the study and discovery of what exists. Guesswork, conjecture, ideas, notions, personal feelings, is not true 'science'! Such notions should have no place in the reporting or publishing of 'scientific' information as being fact, unless clearly stated as such!

The 'Theory of Evolution' is a 'theory'. It is not a fact, but because it is almost universally believed as a fact, most people regard it as such. But it is not.

A look at the word 'theory' helps to acknowledge that all theories are ideas, speculation.

Theory *1590's, "conception, mental scheme," from Late Latin theoria (Jerome), from Greek theoria "contemplation, speculation; a looking at, viewing; a sight, show, spectacle, things looked at," from theorein "to consider, speculate, look at," from theoros "spectator,"*

In other words, 'theories' are things looked at, considered, speculated about, but in no sense at all proven. Guesses! Dear Reader, would you not agree?

So is the 'theory' of Evolution scientific? No, absolutely not. It is supposition and speculation.

The 'science' of today makes nonsense of the 'science' of yesterday.

EVILUTION & SETI 109

This would not be true if only proven facts were released or published by the scientific community.

So many 'scientific' statements and conclusions we read and hear about are stated as 'fact', when in reality they are guesses, theories, extrapolations, and other forms of notional thought. But because they are quoted by a 'scientist', it is expected that they will be accepted as true. Also journalists are prone to exaggerate, dramatise and even falsify reports. A healthy scepticism towards all such pronouncements would not go amiss.

Only eighty years ago, 'science' incorrectly believed that there was only one galaxy, the Milky Way, within which the Earth resides. Now it is known scientifically, that there are as many galaxies as there are billions of stars in the Milky Way!

This simple statement gives one pause for thought, and a question: How do the 'scientists' count the billions of stars in the Milky Way, which is millions of light years across? Or do they just estimate, or perhaps even guess how many there are?

Eighty years ago, children were taught in school how life developed from strings of simple proteins which had assembled themselves from their component parts. These proteins were swimming in what was called then the 'primordial seas'. Quite how that could happen was not explained. Anyway, that was the 'theory', the popular 'science' of that time.

All such statements clearly appeal to the masses, but where is the scientific proof that they are fact? It simply is not there.

Proteins are not simple molecules, but very complex.

One argument put forward by evolutionists suggests that atoms floating in the primordial seas connected themselves together to make 'simple protein'.

Ask on the Internet: 'What is the simplest protein' and here is what you get:-

The simplest of the amino acids, glycine, has just H as an R-group. Amino acids are the structural elements from which proteins are built. When amino acids bond to each other, it is done in the form of an amide , making a connection which is called a peptide linkage.

This is hardly a simple compound, and it is not a protein. Actually, the idea of this item being able to form itself is one thing, but this is an amino acid, not a protein. How many amino acids go to make up the 'simplest' protein? At least 200, and some many more!

The chemical formula of one amino acid called glycine is $C_2H_5NO_2$ (2 Carbon, 5 Hydrogen, 1 Nitrogen, 2 Oxygen), not simple at all, but that is not a protein. Another is $C_3H_7NO_2$, but to make a protein, you have to imagine for example 200 of these amino acids strung together and you have one protein'.

There are countless thousands of different proteins. The idea that this process of stringing all these atoms together in the right order could all happen by chance and of its own accord, is beyond all sense or reason.

Clearly, there is no such thing as a 'simple protein', and such a statement is not only inaccurate, but completely unscientific. And this proposition or assertion is made to support an unsupportable theory.

In that era almost a lifetime ago, children were taught that some of these 'proteins' that had formed themselves were struck by lightning and became 'alive'. This in itself was a strange suggestion, when everybody knows that when anything that is alive is struck by lightning, it dies!

Further, kids then were told that after millions of years, these proteins had formed themselves into creatures which ventured out of the oceans, and developed into breathing land animals. What a fantastic story had been woven by 'scientists'! Complete and utter nonsense, but it was the 'science' of the time.

Now in this 21ˢᵗ Century, despite all our recent discoveries, and our ability to see 'into' the marvels of Creation, mankind still rejects God.

Eighty years ago, the fastest way to make calculations was with a pencil and a piece of paper one at a time. The Orientals had a marvellous gadget called an Abacus. Those who were skilled in its use could make quite complicated calculations quickly, but only one calculation at a time. Even with the invention of the electric calculator, it was faster, but only one calculation at a time could be performed.

Then the computer was invented which could do lots of calculations 'at once'. Now they can make millions or even trillions of calculations each second! This has enabled humans to explore the 'magic' of mathematics and logic to the nth degree.

The Electron Microscope has enabled scientists to look into the almost infinitely small, and see the unimaginable wonders of atoms, molecules, and cell life. The Hubble telescope has enabled astronomers to view the enormity of more of the Universe, uncluttered with the 'fog' of our atmosphere, than they ever knew existed before.

None of this even begins to compare with the awesome Omniscience and computing Power of God! Jesus gave us a glimpse of the enormity of God's Power.

Matthew 10:29 Are not two sparrows sold for a farthing? and one of them shall not fall on the ground without your Father. 30 But the very hairs of your head are all numbered.

God repeats for emphasis in Luke.
Luke 12:6 Are not five sparrows sold for two farthings, and not one of them is forgotten before God? 7 But even the very hairs of your head are all numbered. Fear not therefore: ye are of more value than many sparrows.

There are currently seven billion humans on earth, and God can be aware of the number of hairs on each head! However many sparrows there are, God is aware of each of them if He wishes.

Jesus Christ may have been speaking figuratively, but the literal possibility is clearly there! That would be simple compared to His knowledge of the uncountable galaxies, stars, planets, and heavenly bodies in the expanding Universe which God upholds and sustains with the Word of His Power!

Still today, sadly the notion and belief in an Intelligent Creator God is rejected by most...

Despite all the clear evidence of Intelligent life.

It has been reported recently in this 21st century that a 'synthetic' form of 'life' had been created in a laboratory. By genetic engineering of the smallest, simplest (?) bacteria known, by stripping out the DNA, and replacing it with an artificial man made code, it began to reproduce itself. This is more unscientific nonsense. Notice they started with a form of life, then modified it. So in fact, even if they did do this, they did not create 'life'.

Life can only come from life, and the Source of all life is God.

1 John 5:11 And this is the record, that God hath given to us eternal life, and this life is in his Son.

In the 21st century, teaching the knowledge of God as Creator has largely been eradicated from schools in even the countries which call themselves Christian, and replaced with godless evolutionary notions.

There is still enormous controversy in the school systems about whether everything came about by 'Intelligent Design' or by 'Evolution'

One of the world's most highly educated, respected, well known and celebrated naturalists whose knowledge of the natural world is probably unparalleled, firmly rejects the notion of God, and still apparently supports Darwin's theories. Incredible but true. His television programmes keep his audience of many hundreds of millions around the world entertained by his charm, and astonished at his knowledge, but he is unwittingly misleading them because of his strong personal beliefs.

Since Darwin's day, scientific investigations have repeatedly made unproven 'discoveries' which revealed that much of what 'science' previously thought to be true was not. This gave rise to the truism we repeat:

The 'science' of today makes nonsense of the 'science' of yesterday!

Millions of people around the world are dignified by the term 'scientist'. As time has gone by, so often, shortly after their work is published, in research, other 'scientists' make further discoveries that completely disprove what was previously claimed to be true. Hence the 'truism' quoted above.

DID EVERYTHING REALLY COME FROM NOTHING?

The ultimate sacrilegious insanity is to give credit to the creation of all matter, by insisting that it created itself.

Some 'Theoretical Astro-Physicists' have apparently suspended a basic law of physics which simply states: 'For every cause there is an effect' which used to be taught to children in school.

Apparently this definition no longer matches 'scientists' modern ideas and concepts because they have a new version of this law which now proposes that: 'Though there is a cause and effect relationship, one must ask, if there is more than one cause that has produced any given effect', or that 'one cause may give rise to multiple effects'. That statement is not at all easy for a lay person to understand, if indeed they can work out what it means.

So why do so many scientists think that everything came from nothing? It seems that they do. Why, it is because they have rejected God as Paul says once again in Romans.

Romans 1:21 Because that, when they knew God, they glorified him not as God, neither were thankful; but became vain in their imaginations, and their foolish heart was darkened. 22 Professing themselves to be wise, they became fools,

How did they become fools? By rejecting the Glory of God, instead they have made a vain and empty theory into a 'god' of their own invention, which they worship.

Romans 1:23 And changed the glory of the uncorruptible God into an image made like to corruptible man, and to birds, and fourfooted beasts, and creeping things.

This theory rejects the truth of Creation, and substitutes a lie in its stead.

Romans 1:25 Who changed the truth of God into a lie, and worshipped and served the creature more than the Creator, who is blessed for ever. Amen.

The current 'scientific' stated view of how everything we know of came to be, might be an idea for a fairytale, but is hardly scientific. Their statement is based on another modern unproven notion which simply put states:

"Once upon a time, there was nothing. No space, no matter, nothing at all. Then, 13.7 billions years ago, there was the 'Big Bang'".

Simple question: If there was nothing, what went bang? This very idea also contradicts another absolute 'law of human physics' that:-

'Matter and energy cannot be created or destroyed but can only be changed from one state to another'.

Since there is a 'law' that matter cannot be created or destroyed, then to suggest that there was 'nothing' and then there was 'something' does not make any sense at all.

Anyway, moving along, the story goes, "As a result of the 'Big Bang', space was formed which was full of hydrogen gas." (They do not say what caused this process, or where the hydrogen gas came from.)

Nor can they explain the fact that each atom of hydrogen is 99.99999% empty space, but contains a nucleus and an electron fuelled by energy which moves continuously in orbits.

Where does that energy inside an atom come from? Some say electromagnetic fields, but where do they come from?

Here is a most appropriate place to quote from the Word of the Almighty God who created the heavens and the earth and all that in them is, including our brains and minds, and all the laws partially defined by the so-called science of 'physics' that man likes to think he devised.

*Ecclesiastes 8:17 Then I beheld all the work of God, that a man **cannot find** out the work that is done under the sun: because though a man labour to seek it out, yet he shall not find it; yea farther; **though a wise man think to know it, yet shall he not be able to find it.***

The minds of those who reject God also reject His Word, the Holy Bible, which is the **only** source of the basic physical and spiritual truths by which we are successfully to conduct our lives that we humans need to understand.

The 'Electromagnetic Spectrum' is a range of frequencies from very low 'ELF's', to audible sound from 18 to about 20,000 cycles/second. It continues on. Forty 'octaves' above that is the narrow 'window' of the 'ROYGBIV', the red, orange, yellow, green, blue, indigo, violet light colours of the rainbow. Then continue on up to extremely high x-rays and cosmic rays.

The source of the 'Electromagnetic Spectrum' is inexplicable if one denies the existence of the Creator God and His Power. Where did it come from, how is it there? Modern science cannot explain where it came from, or how it began.

God created Light, a tiny section of the 'Electromagnetic Spectrum' and sustains the whole spectrum, as He does all His invisible Laws that give substance to His Creation.

1 John 1:5 This then is the message which we have heard of him, and declare unto you, that God is light, and in him is no darkness at all.

There is still some variant views about light being either a wave, or particles, or photons, or all of the above, and that it may or may not travel at 'the speed of light' or in a straight line all the time! When God says humans cannot completely fathom His Works, He means it!

These 'Theoretical Physicists' are some of the most intelligent and the most highly educated people on the planet. One of them states, "The hero of the Big Bang was gravity." It was gravity that immediately got to work on the hydrogen atoms to influence them to get together and form spheres. How? He does not say.

To be clear, the whole proposal of the 'Big Bang' theory happening all of itself presupposes the pre-existence of all the so-called 'laws of physics' such as these: Energy, Gravity, Centrifugal Force, the Electromagnetic Spectrum, Radiation, Magnetism, Electricity, and so on.

No scientist can explain the origin of these energies. The reason for that is that they are all emanations of the Power of God Who they reject.

All Energy comes from God who is the Source of all Power. In denying God, they are giving credit to those Laws and all that Matter for forming themselves, which is insane. As already said, it is also sacrilegious in the sense that they steal all the credit for creating the breathtaking wonders of the Universe from the Almighty God.

If Christians have objections to the Big Bang theory, those objections should only be to the atheistic presuppositions that often go along with some who proclaim the theory.

The idea itself that the universe came into existence, and was created due to an explosion (of God's Power) is not necessarily incompatible with the biblical creation account. As one Christian theologian has stated, "I am not necessarily opposed to the Big Bang theory. Rather, I know Who banged it." God did.

Life can only come from life

The 'Theory of Evolution' is widely accepted as fact. It is not fact, it is an empty, false theory based on the contradiction of the law of Biogenesis known to most scientists of Biology. That Law is that "Life can only come from Life". However no human being can explain exactly what 'life' is, or how it came to be on Earth.

Evolution claims that the first 'life' came from inanimate lifeless protein chains which had combined themselves from their component atoms floating in the primordial seas. They do not explain the presence of oceans. This proteinatious matter sprang into life when struck by lightning! Lightning is not well known for creating life, rather it destroys any life it hits.

Organic chemistry is the branch of science that is involved with all living matter. **Organic chemistry** involves the study of the structure, properties, and preparation of complex chemical compounds that consist primarily of carbon and hydrogen. The element Carbon miraculously exists in many forms from the softest soot to the hardest diamond, how this came about is not explained by God rejecting 'scientists'.

Water is a compound made from two gases, Hydrogen and Oxygen. Yet when bound together, two gases form water, without which life is impossible. Miraculous! Water is unusual in that it can exist as a solid as ice, liquid, or as a gas, vapour. Water is also very unusual in that it has a 'memory' the capacity to retain information.

It has been effectively demonstrated by God respecting scientists that water can record and even retain impressions of spiritual matters, like love and hate, order and chaos. It is to be wondered whether there has ever been any attempt to understand how this happens.

Some quotes from an 'authority' on evolution
Here are a few quotes from the soundtrack of a TV documentary that presents a godless evolutionary, self-creating Universe. It features a much loved 'star', a professor of astro-physics who has a huge following:

He says, *"It is a fact, and one of the great mysteries of our Universe that everything is made out of a few simple building blocks that interact with each other according to a few simple laws of Nature. And that applies to everything, stars planets and galaxies, rocks and oceans, but also living things. That raises an intriguing possibility, by looking carefully at Nature, by doing science, we might be able to understand what life is, and perhaps how it began."*

Comment: The 'building blocks' are not simple. Each atom of every substance is a miracle of Energetic Engineering, God's secret method of Creation.

Deuteronomy 29:29 The secret things belong unto the Lord our God: but those things which are revealed belong unto us and to our children for ever, that we may do all the words of this law.

He also states: *"The origin of life is one of the great unsolved scientific mysteries. Its origins seem to be lost in the mists of time.*

Comment: The origins of life are not lost in the mists of time. If you have a Bible, you have the simple story in your hand that will unravel the mystery. God created and gave life. All it takes is a little belief in God, a little faith, and a good measure of humility.

He suggests: *"In common with many scientific mysteries, there may be answers, if you ask simple questions. Why does a moth go to a flame? The deepest question you can ask about a moth is 'How did it come to exist in the first place?'"*

Comment: He poses a 'simple' question in the same paragraph as a 'deepest' question. Again the Holy Scriptures explain the mechanism of Creation. God designed it all, every last atom of it, then He created it all. That story is a lot easier to grasp and believe, than to suggest that everything made itself.

"We don't go back to the origin of life on Earth; we don't have a time machine."

Comment: 'We' meaning scientists, cannot go back to the origin of life, even if they claim it happened 13.2 billion years ago, that can only be a theory, a guess.

"But we do have the moth, and these are like little history books. Their story of four billion years is written into every cell of its body."

Comment: Cute analogy, but not really. A very appealing thought, and indeed the Glory of God, and His amazing Creative Power are built into every cell of a moth's body.

"In order to discover the 'spark' of life, we just have to learn to read the book."

Comment: Scientists and every human being, already struggle with the inability to 'read' the 'Book' properly, not the 'moth'! If only they would allow God to explain how to 'read' His Book, he would and He does. In the Scriptures, God explains how He gives the 'spark of life' to all 'life', and tells the reader how He does it.

"So we have to break the problem down into simple questions. What are the ingredients of 'Life'? How is life formed from such simple ingredients? And what was the driving force, the energy force that ignited the flame four billion years ago? For the first five hundred million years of history, there was no life (fact or guesswork?), just the volcanic violence of a young planet subjected to the bombardment of countless meteorites from space. "

Comment: Scientists know the ingredients, the atoms and molecules that make up all living things, but they do not know what the 'Life Force' is, because they will not give credit to the One who ignited it who **is** the 'Force'. Even some science fiction writers get closer to understanding that!

"But somehow, somewhere, the ingredients of the planet were transformed, and inanimate became animate, and once ignited, that spark has never been extinguished. "

Comment: All right, 'somehow', 'somewhere', inanimate became animate'. In truth, scientists know it is impossible for 'life' to occur spontaneously, they have never seen it happen. They know that the Law of 'biogenesis' real. So why make the statement?

"We are searching for our ancestor from a time when there was no life. "

Comment: Our 'Ancestor' is communicating with us now if only we can recognise it. God's Book is written in His language, and it is not at all easy for the carnal mind to understand. But with the help of Holy Spirit, the story emerges step by step to those who take the time to study earnestly.

We can all pray that one day people with such brilliant human minds will humble themselves to do just that.

God is Spirit, He is the Source of all forms of 'life'
Many human beings, including some scientists resist the concept that "Life can only come from Life", but the evidence is self evident in all life forms we know. This mental resistance comes from the fact that basic human nature is at war with even the idea of God.

God is Life, and is the only Source and the Origin of all life. Human beings have little control over life. Once extinguished, 'life' cannot be brought back or reinstated by human efforts.

God gives 'life' to all living matter in the form of 'quickening' spirit essence, a part of His 'spirit'. When God takes that spirit away 'life' ceases.

John 6:63 It is the spirit that **quickeneth***; the flesh profiteth nothing: the words that I speak unto you, they are spirit, and they are life.*

Quickeneth: quicken (v) c. 1300, "come to life; give life to," from quick (adj.) + en. Meaning "become faster" is from 1805.

The book of Job is the oldest book of the Bible.

Job 33:4 The spirit of God hath made me, and the breath of the Almighty hath given me life.

There is a 'spirit in man' and a 'spirit' in all animal life. The 'spirit in man' enables humans to have knowledge, understanding, and wisdom, and the ability to be in touch with God, which animals do not have.

Job 32:8 But there is a 'spirit' in man: and the inspiration of the Almighty giveth them understanding.

The 'spirit' in a camel, or a dog, or a pig, or a bird, or a whale gives these animals the living force to be what they are and defines their mental state.

When they die, that 'spirit in man', and the 'spirit' in all living creatures return to God who gave it when they took their first breath.

Ecclesiastes 12:7 Then shall the dust return to the earth as it was: and the spirit shall return unto God who gave it.

Modern 'scientists' with all their vast knowledge, information that was completely unknown in Paul's day, or for that matter in Darwin's time, are still aptly described by Christ through Paul in Romans.

Romans 1:18 For the wrath of God is revealed from heaven against all ungodliness and unrighteousness of men, who hold (back) the truth in unrighteousness; 19 Because that which may be known of God is manifest in them; for God hath shewed it unto them.

How did God show it to them? With all the technology available to them in the 21st Century, through the electron microscope, scientists are able to observe the incredible detail of DNA and with 'Hubble' many other wonders of His Creation. But they choose not to give credit to God for the amazing intricate detail of the very small, or the magnificence of the vast expanding Universe, and of His Creation, and His sharing of 'life'.

*Romans 1:20 For the **invisible** things of him from the creation of the world are clearly seen, being understood by the things that are made, even his eternal power and Godhead; so that they are without excuse:*

So what are 'the invisible things' of God?

They are all the manifestations of God Power that are not visible. We listed Energy, Gravity, Magnetism, Electricity, Radiation, The Electromagnetic Spectrum; the Power and motion of protons, electrons and other particles inside atoms, and so on. Evolutionists call these the 'Laws of Physics', and claim that they were the 'cause' of the development of everything that exists. But they are not the 'laws of physics', they are the 'Laws of Almighty God'.

Romans 1:21 Because that, when they knew God, they glorified him not as God, neither were thankful; but became vain in their imaginations, and their foolish heart was darkened.

They could know God, all the evidence is there, but have chosen to worship the god of 'science falsely so-called', and empty, vain imaginations of their own limited minds.

1 Timothy 6:20 O Timothy, (and all Christians today!) keep that (God's Word) which is committed to thy trust, avoiding profane and vain babblings, and oppositions of science falsely so called.

Even in Paul's day, much of the 'science' of the day was known to be false by those who had God's Spirit, and who had the resulting sound mind.

Romans 1:22 Professing themselves to be wise, they became fools,

How? By saying or claiming God does not exist.

Psalm 14:1 The fool hath said in his heart, There is no God. They are corrupt, they have done abominable works, there is none that doeth good.

Scientific thinking concerning the Creation is corrupted by false logic, assumptions, and emotions. If computer files are even slightly 'corrupted' they become unusable.

Conclusions of science based on false premises have to be false, that is scientific!

Romans 1:23 And changed the glory of the uncorruptible God into an image made like to corruptible man, and to birds, and fourfooted beasts, and creeping things.

Our world and the Universe represent the Glory of God. In a sense, they *are* God, at least a part of Him. When evolutionists insist that creatures evolved under their own power over billions of years, they change that 'Glory' into a physical image of their own devising.

Romans 1:25 Who changed the truth of God into a lie, and worshipped and served the creature more than the Creator, who is blessed for ever. Amen.

The Truth is that God Created all things; the Lie is that He did not.

Did everything really come from nothing? This is a ridiculous proposition. No sane person would suggest that anything can come from nothing. When magicians or conjurers make it seem that something has come from nothing, we absolutely know that it had to be a trick.

The Truth of God is that He is the Creator, but Evolutionists worship their own intellect and the notional creative abilities of the creatures they say developed all by themselves, and ignore God. That is idolatry plain and simple.

*Romans 1:28 And even as they did not like to retain God in their knowledge, God gave them over to a **reprobate** (96) **mind** (3563), to do those things which are not **convenient** (2520);*

Reprobate *(96) ajdo>kimov, — ad-ok'-ee-mos; from (1) (a) (as a negative particle) and (1384) (do>kimov); unap-*

proved, i.e. rejected; by implication worthless (literal or moral): — castaway, rejected, reprobate.

Mind *(3563) nou~v, — nooce; probably from the base of (1097) (ginw>skw); the intellect, i.e. mind (divine or human; in thought, feeling, or will); by implication meaning: — mind, understanding.*

Convenient *(2520) kaqh>kw, — kath-ay'-ko; from (2596) (kata>) and (2240) (h[kw); to reach to, i.e. (neuter of presumed active participle, figurative as adjective) becoming: — convenient, fit.*

We Christians, who know that we are the Children of the Creator God, are incredibly privileged to have His Spirit flowing through our repentant sound minds as we feed daily on His Word.

*2 Timothy 1:7 For God hath not given us the spirit of fear; but of **power (1411)**, and of love, and of a **sound mind (4995)**.*

Power (1411) du>namiv, — doo'-nam-is; from (1410) (du>namai); force (literal or figurative); specially miraculous power (usually by implication a miracle itself): — ability, abundance, meaning, might (-ily, -y, -y deed), (worker of) miracle (-s), power, strength, violence, might (wonderful) work.

Sound mind (4995) swfronismo>v, — so-fron-is-mos'; from (4994) (swfJroni>zw); discipline, i.e. self-control: — sound mind.

We rejoice that His Spirit, the Power of God enlightens us, and helps us to reject these ridiculous ideas, and have been given the Gift of more understanding to worship and love the One true God

Ephesians 1:17 That the God of our Lord Jesus Christ, the Father of glory, may give unto you the spirit of wisdom and revelation in the knowledge of him: 18 The eyes of your understanding being enlightened; that ye may know what is the hope of his calling, and what the riches of the glory of his inheritance in the saints, 19 And what is the exceeding greatness of his power to us-ward who believe, according to the working of his mighty power,

Theoretical astro-physicists now have this different 'fairytale' story. They do not start with the evidence of life in all its forms like Darwin did. They have a new idea, a new 'explanation' of how everything we know of came to be. One 'theoretical physicist' (i.e. a 'scientific' physicist who guesses!) states dogmatically that the beginning happened like this repeated here:

Once upon a time, 13.7 billion years ago, there was nothing, no space, no matter, no elements, no nothing.

Then there was a 'Big Bang'.

(Question: If there was nothing, what went bang?)

Immediately after the 'Big Bang' within microseconds, there was space.

The space was filled with Hydrogen.

According to this well known and popular 'scientist', 'Everything came from nothing'. If anyone claimed that an illusionist on stage could actually produce something, or anything from nothing, they would think that person insane.

Remember, this man also says, "The 'hero' of the 'Big Bang' was 'gravity'", because it was 'gravity' that immediately started to act on the Hydrogen atoms to cause them to form spheres, and 'gravity' slowly compressed the Hydrogen to form stars and galaxies of stars.

EVILUTION & SETI

The Internet Wikipedia says: *Gravity, or gravitation, is a natural phenomenon by which all things with mass are brought toward one another, including planets, stars and galaxies, and other physical objects. Since energy and mass are equivalent, all forms of energy cause gravitation and are under the influence of it*

The best that an encyclopaedia can come up with is that 'gravity' is 'a natural phenomenon, one that occurred 'naturally'. How??? The wonders of 'Nature' are actually the wonders of God. Again, 'Mother Nature' gets the credit, not God, and that is another form of idolatry.

Phenomenon: *1570s, "fact, occurrence," from Late Latin phænomenon, from Greek phainomenon "that which appears or is seen," noun use of neuter present participle of phainesthai "to appear," passive of phainein "bring to light, cause to appear, show" (from PIE root *bha- (1) "to shine"). Meaning "extraordinary occurrence" first recorded 1771. Plural is phenomena.*

How gravity forms Hydrogen into spheres is not explained. Nor is the development of the 'Periodic Table' of ninety-two elements explained, but it cannot be, because they did not develop from nothing, they were Created.

We repeat what was said previously for emphasis: 'Scientists' have no explanation as to what Gravity is. They know what it does, they can measure it, they know it is a 'force' related to the size of a mass, but they do not know what that 'force' is, or how it originated. It is not only invisible, it is unfathomable. God made sure that the minds of humankind would be limited compared to His, and would never be able to explain His Powers.

To repeat, nor can they explain any of what they call the 'Laws of Physics: Magnetism, Electricity, Gravity,

Centrifugal Force, Inertia, Radiation, the Electromagnetic Spectrum, Polarity, the Periodic Table, or the Energy in sub-atomic particles…

There is a simple reason for this inability fully to understand them or their origin, which of course, few would accept.

All these Laws concerning Energy are **not** the 'Laws of Physics'. They are the Laws of the Almighty God who is the Source of all Energy, and the Creator of all things through the Creative Power He invested in His Son, Jesus Christ.

Here are a few statements from the Bible, the Book that God wrote.

*John1:1 In the beginning was the Word (or the 'Rock' of the Old Testament who became Christ), and the Word was with God, and the Word was God. 2 The same was in the beginning with God. 3 **All things were made by him; and without him was not any thing made that was made. 4 In him was life**; and the life was the light of men. 5 And the light shineth in darkness; and the darkness comprehended it not… 14 And the Word was made flesh, and dwelt among us, (and we beheld his glory, the glory as of the only begotten of the Father,) full of grace and truth.*

Here in just a few sentences, God the Father tells us how everything was made through His Son Christ Jesus. The 'Jesus Christ' pictured by 'Churchianity' does not fit the fact that through the Father, it was Christ created all things. Again:

Colossians 1:15 (Jesus Christ) Who is the image of the invisible God, the firstborn of every creature:16 For by him were all things created, that are in heaven, and that are in earth, visible and invisible, whether they be thrones, or dominions, or principalities, or powers: all things were created by him, and for him: 17 And he is before all things, and by him all things consist.

By Christ, all things consist, that is everything we know about or will discover.

Hebrews 1:1 God, who at sundry times and in divers manners spake in time past unto the fathers by the prophets, Hath in these last days spoken unto us by his Son, whom he hath appointed heir of all things, by whom also he made the worlds;

God says His Son made the worlds. It is not reasonable or logical that everything appeared by magic from nothing.

Everything was not made out of 'nothing', but God through His Son, converted His Spirit Material into all Energy and Matter that exists. This is the reason that neither Energy nor Matter can be destroyed, because God cannot be destroyed.

This is so simple if anyone will 'allow' God to exist.

Because human beings deny the existence of God, and refuse to believe His Words, that our minds are not capable of understanding the Nature of God, nor finding out about everything that God has made and is Sustaining, they will never be able to work it all out.

*Ecclesiastes 3:12 He hath made every thing beautiful in his time: also he hath set the world in their heart, so that **no man can find out the work that God maketh** from the beginning to the end.*

God has created the world in such a way, and so constructed our minds (hearts) that it is impossible for us to find out or understand the Works of God from start to finish. If only the 'educated' community would take this clear statement from Our Father to heart, and believe it, that would save an awful lot of time and effort.

Especially in regards to the wonders of the stars and galaxies now visible through the man-made miracle of the Hubble telescope. Many thousands of years ago, God wrote in the Bible of stars and constellations

Job 9:9 Which maketh Arcturus, Orion, and Pleiades, and the chambers of the south. 10 Which doeth great things past finding out; yea, and wonders without number.

Nearly six thousand years ago when the Bible was written, God inspired Job to write about the movements of stars and constellations in the heavens which were known to, and observed by the people of the time.

The Hubble telescope has enabled a fantastic view of the heavens never seen before in such detail, but still they struggle with grasping the complexity and enormity of the universe. And most of them, sadly, deny the Designer.

God says: *Isaiah 42:5 Thus saith God the LORD, he that created the heavens, and stretched them out; he that spread forth the earth, and that which cometh out of it; he that giveth breath (life) unto the people upon it, and spirit (of understanding) to them that walk therein:*

Interesting in this ancient text, it says that God not only created the heavens, but 'stretched them out'. Modern astronomers have now come to think that the Universe is constantly expanding (or stretching out?). God told us that thousands of years ago!

*Genesis 1:1 In the beginning God **create**d the heaven and the earth.*

The book of Job is the oldest book in the Bible. Job was a great man. Some suggest that he might have been the architect of the pyramids. God had to teach him some lessons about humility, which could very well apply to many people today who think they now know all about the beginning of things. Here is an example:

Job 38:1 Then the LORD answered Job out of the whirlwind, and said, 2 Who is this that darkeneth counsel by words without knowledge? 3 Gird up now thy loins like a man; for I will demand of thee, and answer thou me. 4 Where wast thou when I laid the foundations of the earth? declare, if thou hast understanding. 5 Who hath laid the measures thereof, if thou knowest? or who hath stretched the line upon it? 6 Whereupon are the foundations thereof fastened? or who laid the corner stone thereof; 7 When the morning stars sang together, and all the sons of God shouted for joy? 8 Or who shut up the sea with doors, when it brake forth, as if it had issued out of the womb 9 When I made the cloud the garment thereof, and thick darkness a swaddlingband for it, 10 And brake up for it my decreed place, and set bars and doors, 11 And said, Hitherto shalt thou come, but no further: and here shall thy proud waves be stayed? 12 Hast thou commanded the morning since thy days; and caused the dayspring to know his place;

Job was clearly deeply affected with the fact that God spoke to him personally, and let him know how small he was compared with the Creator. God continues to reveal His Greatness in all of Creation to Job all through the next several chapters until Job finally says:

Job 42:1 Then Job answered the LORD, and said, 2 I know that thou canst do every thing, and that no thought can be withholden from thee. 3 Who is he that hideth counsel without knowledge? therefore have I uttered that I understood not; things too wonderful for me, which I knew not.

This might be a statement that some 'scientists' and many others might want to utter one day, and lead them to want to echo Job's penitent words which follow:

Job 42:5 I have heard of thee by the hearing of the ear: but now mine eye seeth thee. 6 Wherefore I abhor myself, and repent in dust and ashes.

It is still called 'The Theory of Evolution' by the majority of people in the world. They, and many 'scientists' in the 21st century do 'know' that it is not a proven theory, but still accept it or present it as if it is a fact.

Darwin knew nothing about the structure of the atom, or about DNA, and nothing of the inner workings of single celled creatures. He made simplistic observations, and confused diversity and adaptive changes within species as his basis for supposing that **one species can develop into another which has never been shown to be true**.

This definition from Wikipedia, is a correct statement in that 'evolution' is neither science, nor scientific. It says that **'Evilution is merely an unproven theory'**. The fact that perhaps the majority of human beings believe it to be 'fact' does not make it fact.

The reason Evilution is only a 'theory' is because it certainly cannot be proved 'scientifically' because it is based on two false premises.

1. That there is no God, no Creator.

2. That everything made and developed itself by its innate ability to do so.

These are 'EVIL' statements, because they ignore God.

Dictionary definitions of the word 'science' vary considerably.

Etymologically the word 'science' comes from Middle English, *knowledge, learning*, from Old French, from Latin scientia, from sciēns, scient-, present participle of scīre, *to know*;

Science comes to 'know' by various systems of study:

The definition of 'science' is 'Knowledge or a system of knowledge covering general truths or the operation of general laws especially as obtained and tested through the scientific method'.

'Science' is the observation, identification, description, experimental investigation, and theoretical explanation of phenomena: new advances in science and technology.

Science *claims to be devoted to 'knowing' or 'knowledge' as distinguished from ignorance or misunderstanding'. If only that were true in reality.*

GOD IS

John 4:24 **God is** *a* **Spirit***: and they that worship him must worship him in* **spirit** *and in truth.*

God is not everywhere, but His energy and Spirit is everywhere. God lives in His heaven. God has form and shape and texture, a head, arms, torso, legs, and sits on a throne.

God talks to us through His Word, in His own style of language. He tells us how we can know Who He is.

Romans 1:18 For the wrath of God is revealed from heaven against all ungodliness and unrighteousness of men, who hold the truth in unrighteousness; 19 Because that which may be known of God is manifest in them; for God hath shewed it unto them. 20 For **the invisible things of him** *from the creation of the world are clearly seen, being understood by the things that are made, even his eternal power and Godhead; so that they are without excuse:*

And why are those who do not believe in God, or give Him credit for all things without excuse? Because the tangible evidence of God, and the Intelligent Life that He Created is to be seen everywhere and in everything.

What are the 'invisible' things of God? We repeat with no apology: All types of power are expressions of God and are invisible:-

God's Spirit, Love, life, human spirit, animal spirit, gravity, centrifugal force, magnetism, electricity, the electromagnetic spectrum, *(including light which is an expression of God's Power, 1 John 1:5 This then is the message which we have heard of him, and declare unto you, that God is light, and in him is no darkness at all.)*, the energy within all atoms in the universe that causes the particle(s) within it to orbit, radiation, magnetism, electricity, nuclear power, are all expressions of God's Power, and are invisible. All these Energies and the physical Creation is the evidence that God Is. God says to us:

Isaiah 55:8 For my thoughts are not your thoughts, neither are your ways my ways, saith the LORD. 9 For as the heavens are higher than the earth, so are my ways higher than your ways, and my thoughts than your thoughts.

Again:

*Deuteronomy 29:29 The **secret things** belong unto the Lord our God: but those **things** which are revealed belong unto us and to our children for ever, that we may do all the words of this la*w.

What are the 'secret things' that belong to God? They are everything about Him that He chooses **not** to reveal to us. Like how God's energy has the Power to create matter out of His Spirit. Or how God's Power can uphold, sustain, and maintain everything that is, all things that exist through Christ.

Hebrews 1:3 Who being the brightness of his glory, and the express image of his person, and upholding all things by the word of his power, when he had by himself purged our sins, sat down on the right hand of the Majesty on high:

God has placed restrictions on His human children, so that His secrets stay with Him, and are past finding out.

Romans 11:33 O the depth of the riches both of the wisdom and knowledge of God! how unsearchable are his judgments, and his ways past finding out!

Human arrogance thinks it can 'prove' this Scripture wrong. Not so!

*Ecclesiastes 3:11 He hath made every thing beautiful in his time: also he hath set the world in their heart, **so that no man can find out the work that God maketh from the beginning to the end.***

God 'set the world in our hearts'. That is, God made our minds, and our 'grey matter' so that it is just not equipped completely to comprehend the 'work of God', the Creation. Our minds were not designed to be able to work it all out. God repeats many statements in His Word, particularly when He wants to emphasise something.

*Ecclesiastes 8:17 Then I beheld all the work of God, that a man **cannot find** out the work that is done under the sun: because though a man labour to seek it out, **yet he shall not find it; yea farther; though a wise man think to know it, yet shall he not be able to find it.***

So when human beings attempt to make sense of everything that is, but leave God out of the picture, they lose themselves in the insanity and vanity of their own minds. They embrace instead the godless notion of Evolution, even suggesting that the miracle of 'life' comes from inanimate objects.

All 'Life' is a gift from God Who Is Life, and once 'life' is withdrawn cannot be revived. A baby grows inside its mother using part of her life force, and does not become an independent individual until it is born and takes its first breath, and with that breath, its human 'spirit' of life from God. And people deny God exists. That is wilful ignorance. We repeat what Christ inspired Paul to write:

Romans 1:21 Because that, when they knew God, they glorified him not as God, neither were thankful; but became vain in their imaginations, and their foolish heart was darkened. 22 Professing themselves to be wise, they became fools, (who say there is no God) 23 And changed the glory of the uncorruptible God into an image made like to corruptible man, and to birds, and fourfooted beasts, and creeping things... 25 Who changed the truth of God into a lie (evolution), and worshipped and served the creature more than the Creator, who is blessed for ever. Amen.

Let those who think they are 'wise' while denying God and thus making themselves 'fools', consider that God could be there for even them.

Jeremiah 9:23 Thus saith the LORD, Let not the 'wise' man (who thinks he is wise!) glory in his wisdom, neither let the mighty man glory in his might, let not the rich man glory in his riches: 24 But let him that glorieth glory in this, that he understandeth and knoweth me, that I am the LORD which exercise lovingkindness, judgment, and righteousness, in the earth: for in these things I delight, saith the LORD.

That says it all really!

SETI

THE SEARCH FOR INTELLIGENT LIFE ON OTHER PLANETS

The sad search for intelligent life, Humans looking in the wrong direction!

The Search for Extra-Terrestrial Intelligence (SETI) is an exploratory science that seeks evidence of intelligent life in the universe by looking and listening into space for some "signature" of its technology.

Extra-terrestrial Intelligence is here on Earth in everything we know.

SETI will not get radio evidence of extra-terrestrial intelligence; they are looking in the wrong direction! The evidence of Supreme Intelligence is all around them right here on Earth. Everything that there is, and that we know about, can observe and measure is the result of amazing, incredible Design and Intelligence of God's Power.

Everything is Energy and the result of Energy Intelligently used to Create what we know. The 'Laws of Physics' that they rely on to do their extraordinary feats of engineering are not the 'Law of Physics' at all.

Those Laws are expressions of the Energy Laws of the Almighty God!

People have a deep-seated fear of being alone.

Human beings are not alone, God Who made us is with us, is part of us, and in everything that exists, all is an expression of His Power. He is with us whether we believe it or not.

The only reason people are searching for extra-terrestrial beings is because they feel alone because they reject God as the Creator of all things, and are blind to His Power and what He has made. As human beings, we have five physical senses:

Seeing, Hearing, Taste, Smell and Touch

These are the physical senses used by humans, including scientists, in their search for understanding. The reason their understanding is so limited, is because they are missing the 'sixth sense'. People speak of a 'sixth sense'. The dictionary defines it as:

Sixth Sense. The dictionary says is, *"a power of perception like but not one of the five senses: a keen intuitive power"*

We need to understand clearly what the 'sixth sense' is.

Because **physical** human beings are given a **'spirit in man'** at birth, that spirit we retain all our lives until we die, that 'spirit' can witness with God's Spirit. This empowers our minds, so that we can know some things 'intuitively'.

Romans 8:16 The Spirit itself beareth witness with our spirit, that we are the children of God:

Some people use 'their own' intuition to know how to act, in healing for instance, which could be very unreliable. However we need to discern the nature of any spiritual activity we might experience, and not be gullible.

1 Timothy 4:1 Beloved, believe not every spirit, but try the spirits whether they are of God: because many false prophets are gone out into the world.

What does it mean to 'try' the spirits? The word 'try' in Greek means 'to test'. We need to be cautious and check out any feelings of 'knowing' anything or something to make sure that it is consistent with God's Word, and never just trust our own 'intuition'.

The word in-tuition could be said to be 'teaching from within'. A lot of people use their 'intuition' to help solve their metaphysical or healing activities. This is good and well, providing they are accessing knowledge and experiences they have learned in life, but are not able consciously to recall. That is, the information they feel they know 'intuitively' comes from their training, something they may have read, or their experiences.

However, it can be dangerous to trust their 'intuition' if the signals or ideas that come up during its use are coming from a source outside themselves. What other 'source' could that be? It could be that under some circumstances, people who think of themselves as 'intuitive' may be using devices like pendulums, ouija boards, or think they can 'channel' dead people to glean information, and thereby opening up their minds to possible interference by 'familiar spirits' which God condemns.

A quick look at 'intuitive' from the dictionary:

Intuition: Literally teaching from within. insight, direct or immediate cognition, spiritual perception," originally theological, from Late Latin intuitionem_ "to perceive directly without reasoning, know by immediate perception"

It says 'intuition' is 'spiritual perception', originally theological. Theological is made up of two words, Theo - God and Logos - Word. Christians do get 'intuition' from God's Word as we study it by the Power of God's Holy Spirit flowing in our minds. It is teaching from Him to within us.

Using our 'sixth sense', our 'spirit' awareness of God, expands our knowledge, understanding, and wisdom.

If we look to God as our Father, He will give us another three spiritual senses:

Knowledge of our Human Spirit,

Awareness of God Who is a Spirit,

and Christ His Son the conduit of Wisdom,

via the Power of God's Holy Spirit.

Scientists, who reject God as Creator, are left to believe the 'theory' that everything created itself and evolved of its own accord over billions of years. This theory is frankly insane, not reasonable, and is unprovable.

When did the idea of SETI begin?

Since the beginning of civilisation, people have wondered if we are alone in the Universe. Over time, there have been many ideas about extra-terrestrial intelligence within our Solar system.

In 1896, Nikola Tesla suggested that an extreme version of his wireless electrical transmission system could be used to contact beings on Mars.

In 1924, during August 21–23rd, Mars came closer to Earth than at any time in the century before. In the United States, a "National Radio Silence Day" during a 36-hour period, with all radios quiet for five minutes on the hour, every hour. At the U.S. Naval Observatory a radio receiver tuned to a wavelength between 8 and 9 km, using a "radio-camera" developed was lifted 3 kilometres (1.9 miles) above the ground in an airship. Nothing came of these experiments but it shows that the idea of looking for 'something out there' certainly is not new.

In the late 1950's, with the advent and development of the Radio Telescope, it became possible for astronomers to listen to the electromagnetic emissions of the universe. Scientists reckoned that extra-terrestrial intelligences would attempt to contact other places where there were other civilisations in the universe, even as we are doing. This is quite an assumption.

In 1960, Cornell University astronomer Frank Drake performed the first modern SETI experiment. Drake used a radio telescope 26 metres (85 ft) in diameter to examine the stars. A 400 kilohertz band was scanned. He found nothing of interest.

In 1967, in an article in *The Flying Saucer Reader*, there was even an idea for a song suggested about SETI. The song was recorded by the Carpenters which became very popular around the world. It was called 'Calling Occupants of Interplanetary Craft'. Here are a few lines of the lyric:

In your mind you have capacities you know
To telepath messages through the vast unknown

Calling occupants of interplanetary, most extraordinary craft
You've been observing our earth

And we'd like to make a contact with you. We are your
friends

The words of this plaintive song were calling out to anyone who might be listening anywhere in space, offering friendship. This epitomised the inherent loneliness so many human beings are aware of or feel.

NASA combined the SETI notions in the late '60's. They had Project Orion, the Microwave Observing Project, and in 1992 NASA initiated a more intensive SETI programme to cost $100 million. Less than a year later Congress cancelled the programme.

Parts of the SETI programme are continuing today with private funding by what is still called the SETI Institute. Founded in 1984, it is a non-profit organisation. The SETI Institute then employed over one hundred scientists, educators and support staff. Its stated mission is to explore, understand and explain the origin, nature and prevalence of life in the universe.

From statements of many of those involved, it seems that the Institute staff approach their studies of Earth's origins from a secular position that excludes the existence of God.

In 1977, The NASA Voyager I & II were sent into space. Billions were spent on this NASA project, which employed thousands of people to design and construct the spacecraft. All these people were clearly very intelligent, highly educated, and qualified in their particular roles. It departed from Cape Canaveral on Aug. 20, 1977 to explore Jupiter and Saturn. Voyager 1 followed a few weeks later and is now ahead of Voyager 2.

In 2017, Sunday August 20th marked the 40th anniversary of NASA's launch of Voyager 2. It is humanity's farthest spacecraft at 13 billion miles away. Voyager is the world's only craft to reach interstellar space, the vast mostly emptiness between star systems. Voyager 2 is almost to the limit of the effect of our Sun's gravity, and is expected to cross that boundary during the next few years.

In 2017, a two part documentary was made giving information on the development, launch, and flight details of the two Voyager spacecraft. In the commentary, many of the scientists who were involved with the development of the original project 40 years ago are now, of course, older men and women. Many gave their feelings about SETI, and why it came about in 1984, and the idea still fascinates many people.

Source of the following statement (with quotes and brackets added) was taken recently from the http://www.seti.org website:

"Our current understanding of life's origin on Earth suggests that given a suitable environment, and sufficient time, life will develop on other planets. Whether "evolution" will give rise to intelligent, technological civilisation is open to speculation. (Yes, it certainly is!) However such a civilisation could be detected across interstellar distances, and may actually offer our best opportunity for discovering extraterrestrial life in the near future."

Notice those words, *'given a suitable environment'*, and *'sufficient time'*, *'life will develop on other planets'*. These statement are based on the 'belief', the 'theory' that life spontaneously developed, or 'evolved' on our planet Earth. The next part of the statement reveals that it is a 'speculation', or 'guess' whether 'evolution' will give rise to intelligent life somewhere in interstellar space.

Comments made by some of the NASA Voyager team.

In 2017, during two hour long documentaries, many scientists made comments, but not one mentioned God. Not one gave credit to the Creator for the wonders of the expanding Universe that has scientists staggered with its vastness. Not one suggested that the Bible might contain any of the answers to all their many questions.

The common thread of all these comments which follow by top scientists are the questions most people have at one time or another:

Are we alone in the Universe?

Is there Intelligent Life out there?

What is the purpose of it all?

With all their knowledge, with all their education, with all their sincere desire to 'know', because they start with the false premise that evolution is a fact, and that there is no God, they are doomed to ignorance.

All they would have to do is to look into God's Word, believe, and have faith that God exists, and they would begin to discover the answer to all their questions. It is so sad that they will not do that.

To those who support the Darwinian notional theory of evolution, SETI seems to be a perfectly logical exercise.

To those who believe in our Creator God, and do not support the concepts of evolution, the whole SETI activity is a fruitless waste of time, money, expertise and resources, which could be better utilised solving or relieving some of our world's worst problems.

Forty years later, some of the many astro-physicists working for NASA on the Voyager I and II spacecraft had these comments to make:

One said: *"Are we alone? I would like to know the answer to that question. There have to be other civilisations. It is just compelling. It would be almost statistically impossible for their not to be other life-forms that have evolved to a state of intelligence and beyond".*

Yet another space scientist said: *"We think we are intelligent, and I think intelligent life is so prevalent I will bet you that in this instant, there are two people probably one male and one female having exactly the same conversation that you and I are having right now. That is how prevalent life is in the universe."*

Another suggested: *"They are probably trying to contact us this very minute. I predict that right now, radio messages are flowing through this room that we could detect with equipment we could build, if we knew where to aim that detector and what frequency to tune to."*

A lady space expert suggested: *"It depends ultimately how long our civilisation lasts, and how long others, last because you have to get them to overlap so they can communicate."*

Another 'theoretical physicist' proposed: *"Our Galaxy is about 12 billion years old, our Sun is rather 'young', only about 4 and a half billion years old, many stars are a lot older than that. Therefore you can imagine a civilisation around another star, that might have watched ours form and the development of ours which has only been going on over the last 4 billion years. The only evidence they would have had over the last sixty or so years would be by watching 'Star Trek' or 'l Love Lucy' signals that we sent out, or whatever, or other programs. Even if someone said look at that star, and look at that third rock from that star, and that is where you will find life, even if they knew which object to look for, there is only a fifty year period out of five billion years almost, where you would find intelligent life on our Earth".*

Another: *"If we are alone, then we are truly... and why us? Why are we so special, and yet in such a far-flung sort of humdrum part of the Universe, and if we are not alone, how do we learn about all those other groups out there, what are they like? Are they creatures of our dreams or nightmares?"*

Yet another says: *"I think what is going to save us is that inter-stellar travel is much harder than we think, and we are safe for quite a long time from the aliens as they don't know how to travel far either, and so we are all kinda stuck on the planets we have got."*

Another space scientist observes: *"Saturn has moons, and the one of greatest of interest is Titan which is the largest, and has some similarities with how Earth was billions of years ago early in our history. Very little Oxygen, many hydrocarbons, a dense thick smoggy atmosphere, which was changed dramatically on our planet by life!! It has a dense Methane atmosphere where complex organic chemistry has been going on for billions of years. Methane, which on Earth is a very flammable gas, is given off by rotting vegetation and when cows break wind. We are in a moment of extraordinary discovery".*

A woman still on the on the Voyager staff says: *"The whole reason and purpose of interplanetary exploration is a story about longing. It is a longing to know ourselves. It is a longing to know the significance of our existence. It is a longing to communicate to the state of the Universe that we are here. You know, know us, where are you?"*

Another scientist asks: *"How would you go about communicating with a totally alien civilisation? The assumption is that we share a similar physical universe. That the laws of Physics applicable here seem to be applicable everywhere. Science and maths are things we could communicate fairly easily. Everyone loves music and pop songs have a simple mathematical structure, but the maths of a Bach Fugue is much more complicated. Mathematics is a universal language, so we put a record of many types of music on board Voyager."*

Another lady space expert says: *"I have concerns. We have intelligent life on our own planet, dolphins, whales, that we cannot communicate with meaningfully apart from fish for tricks. Are we going to meet aliens that we can sit down with to tea together. It is not going to be that simple."*

We are NOT alone! God is with us!

It is really a very tragic fact that none of these people, from their comments, appear to have any knowledge about, or belief in the God of the Bible. If they did, they would realise that far from being 'alone', they are constantly in the Loving Care of their Father in Heaven.

The reality and the clear evidence of 'Extra-Terrestrial Intelligence' is all around us, and in us. We need look no further into outer space, God's Power is everywhere in the Universe, and what matters most to us, His children, is that He is available to us here and now on Earth, as He prepares us for our Glorious future with Him.

Abuse of the 'Laws of Probability' is not scientific.

Given enough time, it has been proposed, anything can make something from nothing. Certainly this is hard for rational people to imagine. If you start with 'nothing', how long does 'nothing' have to be there, to start producing 'something'? Defies logic does it not?

A popular ridiculous suggestion was made some years ago. That if a big enough team of Chimpanzees, each with a typewriter handy, given enough time, would produce the works of Shakespeare. Others suggested that given enough time and enough Scrabble letters, when dropped randomly, would form themselves into a dictionary.

Indeed, some 'scientists' say that given enough time, inorganic elements and energy (from where) could form themselves into molecules which could link into complex proteins. Complex proteins, given the right environment, and enough time, would assemble themselves into primitive (?) cells and spring into life. How?

SETI supporters, like evolutionists think that "given a suitable environment and sufficient time" intelligent civilisations can come from nothing.

How do the "suitable environments" arise? Where do the elements, the energy, the mechanisms come from that form the suitable environments? They have no explanation to offer, and do not seem to address such issues.

I wonder if anyone who holds these notions has ever looked at a single cell under a high powered microscope, and would seriously dare to call it "primitive". A single cell with thousands of component parts, moving itself around with its own 'outboard motor' to propel itself, feeding itself, evacuating its own waste, and reproduces itself. This is primitive?

Watch while a single cell uses it's internal "life energy" (whatever that is, it certainly did not come from nothing!), to reproduce itself, and make two where there was one before. Life can only come from life. Then who could possibly say that cell or the process is "primitive" and that it developed the ability to do that all by itself from lifeless matter without external Intelligence or Design? Most scientists (objective observers?) can and do say that.

They also spend a lot of time and energy in their SETI programmes looking far into space for any signal that will indicate that the source was intelligent. They haven't managed to detect any yet, but they still persist.

Humans have a tendency to 'believe' regardless of fact or truth.

For fifty years in Britain, the government funded a centre to find the viral cause of the common cold. They actually paid people to go there and "catch a cold". After five decades, the centre was closed down, as they had been unable to find any virus that would account for the common cold. That does not stop people from perpetuating the myth to this day.

Yes, today, almost all 'informed' sources will tell you that the common cold is caused by a virus. Never mind the failure of the medical scientific community to determine that such a thing existed, that is irrelevant. Many doctors will still tell you the common cold is caused by a virus.

The common cold is not cause by a virus. It is caused by the need for the body to eliminate toxic material it cannot dispose of via the bladder or the colon. Infections ensue when the bodies' immune system is compromised by having to deal with all the detritus that has built up.

The SETI program is not yielding any results after thirty plus years. Could the reason that the Cold Centre and SETI researchers have not found what they were looking for, is because it does not exist? And are they all looking for extra-terrestrial intelligence in the wrong place? Could it be that there is no need to waste time and money searching the heavens for proof of ETI?

Is the evidence for Intelligence somewhere in outer space right here on the earth? Yes! Does not every part of our surroundings, we humans, the fauna and flora of the Earth all shout the clear evidence that our World could only have been designed and produced by an Intelligent Designer?

Can "Intelligent Life" come from unintelligent nothingness? Does a proposition like that make any sense at all?

What is strange is that the scientific community of this world resist the idea of Intelligent Design in a most unscientific manner. They do not address the issues with a pure investigative, pragmatic, objective approach. They get emotional! Very emotional!!

With all the vast amount of evidence before them, they call those of us who do believe that there was 'Intelligent Design', crazy!

Those who say everything came from nothing, think they are the sane ones, and that people who believe in an Invisible Intelligent God are delusional.

One is surprised that the men in white coats do not come to take them away, ho, ho! The reason they do not, is because this almost universal fierce passion for denying a Prime Cause comes from none other than our God's Adversary. As always, this spirit being, Satan, has very cleverly, got most of the world believing that he does not exist. Satan is hard at work to help keep deceived those hapless souls who know no better than to criticise, ridicule, and deny the truth.

Every tribe and nation has some attachment to their gods, to something greater than themselves. Yet those who believe there was a Prime Cause, an Intelligent Being, a Designer, who uses His power to create, design, and sustain the universes are deemed irrational and insane.

Is that upside down reasoning or what? Those who deny the existence of a God will go to any lengths, rational or irrational to defend their position. What a tragic waste of life's time and energy!

Those who do this, those who reject anything greater than themselves, are not in touch with "The Plan". They are certainly in for a shock. Time is ticking away, and as the saying goes, 'time will tell'. Will their faces become red when they are shown that the position they so cleverly contrived and imposed on others through the world's educational systems, is totally untenable? Will they want to hide?

Will those who have spent years of their lives staring into space, listening to, and analysing meaningless white, pink and other celestial "noise" be embarrassed when they come to realise that the evidence for ETI has been right in front of, and all around them on this Earth all the time? Right under their noses, so to speak!

Will they see the need to 'wash' their minds clean from all their Godless ideas? Will they welcome and embrace the Truths of the Bible?

Psalm 51:2 Wash me throughly from mine iniquity, and cleanse me from my sin.

Isaiah 1:16 Wash you, make you clean; put away the evil of your doings from before mine eyes; cease to do evil;

Proverbs 3:5 Trust in the LORD with all thine heart; and lean not unto thine own understanding. 6 In all thy ways acknowledge him, and he shall direct thy paths. 7 Be not wise in thine own eyes: fear the LORD, and depart from evil.

Will they be prepared to admit they were wrong? Who knows? We can only pray that some will.

CHAPTER 4

THE GREATEST TRUTH – GOD'S WORD

The Bible is the only Book in the world that contains God's Words to us

It is **the** standard text. It is **The** Instruction Book for the Human Race. It is the **only** Book in the world in which God speaks to us in the First Person saying:

"I am God, and there is none other like me."

To be a Christian, it is absolutely essential to have a total conviction that the pages of the Bible we have in our hands contain the absolute Word of God, *the* Truth.

So to be a Christian, we each have a responsibility to ask God to give us the gift of that conviction, and it takes work to prove that to ourselves.

John 17:17 Sanctify them through thy truth: thy word is truth.

How many people, even churchgoers, scientists, others, really believe that?

WHO WROTE THE BIBLE? MEN? OR GOD?

Many people mock the Bible. They say it is full of errors and apparent contradictions. They like to ridicule the book as being a collection of fables and folk lore gathered together by some churchmen in the 300's A.D. They think that these scholars decided what should go into the Bible, and what should not.

Examine for a moment the thinking of most of those people who arrogate to themselves the ability to reject the Book that has survived centuries of attempts to destroy it. The Bible that has had more copies printed than any other Book anytime. Such folk are usually ignorant people, who have never taken the time to study the Book. They just KNOW that the Bible is a bunch of junk. Really?

Then there are the 'scholars' who are atheists who have solid convictions that no God exists; or agnostics who think there is a great deal of doubt and say they do not know. What exactly does 'agnostic' mean? It means a person who professes that the existence of a First Cause, and the essential nature of things, are not, and cannot be known.

This word 'agnostic' was coined in 1870 by T. H. Huxley from Greek *agnostos* "unknown, unknowable." Huxley was an English biologist and was known as "Darwin's Bulldog" for his advocacy of Charles Darwin's theory of Evolution. He did not believe in God, and considered it was not possible to know that God exists.

Then there are religious 'scholars', and 'Theologians', many of whom know Hebrew, Greek, and Aramaic. They pick over the original texts, arguing about this and that issue or doctrine between each other, until they have picked the Scriptures to pieces, and largely missed the beauty of the real message they contain. Not really a scholarly approach!

This author does not just "believe" in God. For him God is a absolute reality. Do you believe in rocks, or buses or aeroplanes? Of course you do not need to. They are there for all to see. Ah! You might say, "But we cannot see God." But we can see what He has created, so we can know and know that we know that He is here with us.

Do you believe that there are other stars and galaxies that you cannot see and have not experienced? The chances are that you would say yes. You know they are here although you have never seen them or experienced them. This is because the evidence that they exist is so overwhelming, that you can KNOW absolutely that they are there.

Now the Hubble telescope, suspended in space, outside the distortion of the Earth's atmosphere, "sees" further and more clearly into space than ever before. The pictures it sends back to Earth confirm that there are ever more things out there than scientists previously thought. So we can really KNOW they are there. Sadly though, it seems that so many of those who use Hubble, although awestruck by what they see, do not give the credit to God, but to Evolution.

The Creation, our World, the Universe is the evidence that there is a God of Infinite Intelligence.
Those who claim that there is no 'Prime Cause' for all matter, say that everything came from 'nothing'. That defies all logic, and frankly, denies rational thinking too. Hopefully chapters two and three might have shed a little light on those theories.

God inspired and created the Scriptures, His Words to His children, to be perfect, and they are.
The Bible is the only Book that claims to have been inspired by God. Writers within its pages say that every word was given by inspiration of God, and under His control was dictated to be written down by men.

Psalm 18:30 As for God, his way is perfect: the word of the Lord is tried: he is a buckler to all those that trust in him.

As a person studies the Bible with the help of Holy Spirit flowing through their mind they will find that the Word is indeed 'tried' and tested, and does not ever contradict itself. God made sure of that.

Let us start with a supposition. There is a God. That God had the power to create all things as we know them. If God created the heavens and the earth, and all that in them is, then that God had some amazing awesome Power.

Imagine you are that God and that you decide to have men write a collection of books, a sort of instruction manual for their conduct on earth. Don't you think that you could manage to inspire those books to be written down by men in exactly the way You wanted it done? Do you imagine that You would allow mere mortal men that You had created and had given life to, to interfere with the presentation of Your Book so that it says what You said and what you wanted it to say?? Of course you would not.

Human beings really are pathetic in their attempts to deny the existence of God. Even the most "scientific" people seem to get emotional and abandon all logical thinking when it comes to anything to do with God.

Why is the Bible so difficult to read?
The Bible is a difficult book to read, and there is a reason for that. God wrote the Bible in His Style and in His particular manner, using His form of language to express the most detailed and complex Spiritual matters. God wrote it to those whose minds are open to receive the truth at any given time.

Religious people may not like to hear it, but God did not write His Book to those whose minds are closed to the Truth at this time. The evidence before us is that apparently most human minds are closed at this time.

The carnal or fleshly human mind, driven by human nature, is incapable of understanding the truths of the Bible in depth.

Romans 8:7 Because the carnal mind is enmity against God: for it is not subject to the law of God, neither indeed can be.

That is right, the human mind is at enmity against God. That means our human carnal minds have a hostile feeling, an internal conflict, and even malice towards the God-given Scriptures. That might sound preposterous, but it is a plain statement that Christ inspired the Apostle Paul to write. So like it or not, it is true. Christ also made this very plain in Matthew.

*Matthew 13:15 For this people's heart is waxed gross, and their ears are dull of hearing, and **their eyes they have closed; lest at any time they should see with their eyes and hear with their ears,** and should understand with their heart, and should be converted, and I should heal them.*

The evidence is all around us, even most people who think they believe in God, and think they love Him, do not understand His Words as you read in chapter two.

God's Spiritual help is needed to understand the Bible properly

Many people think that Jesus Christ spoke in parables, or stories with a meaning, so that the crowds of people who followed Him could understand what He was teaching. This is not so.

Matthew 13:9 Who hath ears to hear, let him hear.

Only those in the crowd who were given 'ears to hear' by Him understood anything. The same is true today. Christ makes it clear that His words were not to be understood by the masses.

Matthew 13:10 And the disciples came, and said unto him, Why speakest thou unto them in parables? 11He answered and said unto them, Because it is given unto you to know the mysteries of the kingdom of heaven, but to them it is not given.

But His disciples still did not understand the meaning of the parables, and had to ask Him to explain it to them, which He did. Those who read the Bible today can read about the meaning of the parables that He taught His disciples, but will not necessarily get the whole depth of meaning, unless they have the 'eyes to see' granted to them provided they ask God for understanding.

Reading the Bible without the help God and His Power of His Holy Spirit serves very little useful purpose. Parts of the Bible contain fascinating stories that are interesting in themselves, but without Holy Spirit flowing in their minds, their deep meaning will be lost on the reader.

The Bible contains Spiritual information that absolutely proves that no man or group of men could possibly have written it. This information about profound Spiritual matters could only have been written by God who is a Spirit.

*John 4:24 **God is** a **Spirit**: and they that worship him must worship him in **spirit** and in truth.*

This is the reason it would have been impossible for any human or group of humans to assemble all the material over centuries. Every student of the Bible needs to prove this fact, and that the Bible is really God's Word to themselves and for themselves. The only way to do that is earnestly to study the Bible, not just read it, but **study** it.

2 Timothy 2:15 Study to shew thyself approved unto God, a workman that needeth not to be ashamed, rightly dividing the word of truth.

What does it mean 'rightly dividing' the word? God wrote the Bible in a complex way. In order to get the complete story, or picture of any topic in the Bible, it is necessary to know that aspects of each topic are sprinkled throughout the Book.

Isaiah 28:10 For precept must be upon precept, precept upon precept; line upon line, line upon line; here a little, and there a little: 11 For with stammering lips and another tongue (God-language) will he speak to this people.

Through Isaiah, God is telling us about His Book and how to access information in it. Precept means 'rule of conduct', or way of thinking, notion or instruction. What these verses mean is that the reader needs to look at a line here, and another line there, gathering little pieces of information through the whole Book to build up a complete picture of any particular subject.

God uses repetition for emphasis in the Bible.
In the Bible, God also very often uses repetition for emphasis of important details. The meaning of the verses in Isaiah 28:10-11 is repeated in verse 13, which adds the fact that the Bible is written like this to make it difficult to understand unless the reader is using God's help.

Isaiah 28:13 But the word of the LORD was unto them precept upon precept, precept upon precept; line upon line, line upon line; here a little, and there a little; that they might go, and fall backward, and be broken, and snared, and taken.

Those that deride and disrespect the truth of God's Word, indeed do 'fall backwards', and are broken and snared', and taken in by the vanity and rebellion of their own minds. Then they complain that the Bible is full of contradictions and old fables. Which it is not.

Also information given in the Bible is not always to be applied universally to all people, or at all times through the centuries. Some information is to certain peoples, and at certain times; other information is applicable at some times and not others. Much confusion is experienced by those who do not understand this principle.

God will guide the earnest student to 'rightly divide' or 'correctly partition' each portion of teaching, so that their understanding of its relevance to them will emerge.

God does not put a funnel into the top of one's head, so to speak, and just pour in all the truth. That would overwhelm anyone. God knows each of us individually, and will give each person all the information that He wants them to know at that time and under the current circumstances in their lives.

The Bible gets a lot of bad publicity.
Here are a few of the type of statements made by ignorant, profane, and uninformed people:

- Men wrote the Bible.

- *No, God wrote the Bible **through** His Servants, Prophets & Apostles*

- The Bible is full of errors and contradictions.
  It is not, the Bible is accurate, and never contradicts itself. However, it is true that all translations into English do contain errors, but with help that need not be a problem to the earnest student.

- All stories in the Bible are fiction, & did not happen
  All the stories contain true principles, whether fact, figurative, or poetic.

- You can prove anything from the Bible.
  That is a nonsense statement made from ignorance

- Scientists and archaeologists have proved the Scriptures false.

No they have not. They may use specious arguments, they may suggest that finds at digs are not consistent with the Bible, but it is correct and they are wrong as one day they will come to realise.

We do not need to give any credence to the critics. They are mere humans, and cannot possibly evaluate God correctly.

2 Timothy 2:16 But shun profane and vain babblings: for they will increase unto more ungodliness.

The word 'profane' from is Latin *profanare, "to desecrate, render unholy, violate". The word 'vain' from Old French vain, means "worthless, void, invalid, feeble; conceited".*

So people who either do not believe in God, or have vague ideas about Him, being at enmity to Him, tend to attack His Word. However, their conceited comments, because of having an overweening opinion of themselves, are both profane and unholy; and vain, feeble, and worthless. How dare they? They fall into some of the categories of the ungodly mentioned in Romans.

Romans 1:30 Backbiters, haters of God, despiteful, proud, boasters, inventors of evil things, disobedient to parents,

'Churchianty' has given God and the Bible a bad name!
Religious people of this world while claiming to be Christian have given God and the Bible a bad name. Religious strife is the root cause of many of the world's wars and problems.

Thousand of churches claiming to be Christian disagree about the meaning of its contents. There cannot be many versions of any Truth. Nor do most churchgoers live the lives of true Christians, many of whom engage in war and other ungodly pursuits that are not consistent with the life God expects Christians to live.

Does the average churchgoer really firmly, passionately believe that the Bible is the Word of God? Do they really study the Bible, or even spend much time even reading it? Unfortunately, most do not. Or is their attitude towards the Holy Scriptures lackadaisical and just the Book they carry to church, or occasionally pick up at home? Our attitude towards the Bible is a measure of our attitude towards God and Christ.

Deuteronomy 6:5 And thou shalt **love** the Lord thy God **with all thine heart**, and **with all thy soul**, and **with all thy might**.

<u>True Christianity is not for the lackadaisical or half-hearted.</u>

Give God the credit for producing a perfect Book
Even to suggest that the Bible is in error, is to fail to give God the credit for being able to produce His Book of instructions to His Children exactly how He wanted it to be.

God and Christ designed and invented the most complex basis for life in the DNA structure of billions of atoms linked in such a way that they form the blueprint for all forms of life. Then He perfectly created the Universe and everything in it.

The accuracy of the timing of all heavenly bodies is more precise than any clock that human beings can devise. The evidence of this perfection may also be observed by careful study of the Scriptures. God says through Christ:

Psalm 8:3 When I consider thy heavens, the work of thy fingers, the moon and the stars, which thou hast ordained; 4 What is man, that thou art mindful of him? and the son of man, that thou visitest him?

We are precious to God, and when we consider the Works of His hands it should provoke us to wonder and praise Him for it all.

Yet secular and religious people cast doubt upon the authenticity of the Bible by pointing out that many years passed between events and the writing of the manuscripts. Christ makes very clear that He ensured that all the writings that were canonised were written under His direction by the Power of the Holy Spirit.

John 14:26 But the Helper, the Holy Spirit, whom the Father will send in My name, He will teach you all things, and bring to your remembrance all things Which I said to you.

We have this promise from Jesus that His disciples, the Apostles, and only those who were witnesses of all that Christ did and said would be given total recall by the Holy Spirit of the things He said and did.

Acts 10:39 And we are **witness**es **of all** things which he did both in the land **of** the Jews, and in Jerusalem; whom they slew and hanged on a tree:

These same disciples either wrote the New Testament books or had input into which works were accepted as Scripture and were included in the Canon, which means 'standard of excellence'.

Any book that claimed canonical status, yet diverted from the truth of the life of Christ, would have been rejected by Jesus' own disciples who were, eyewitnesses to the New Testament events. Thus the acceptance of God's people is an important criterion for a book to be considered canonical.

The word 'canon' in classical Latin means a "measuring line, rule," from Greek *kanon* "any straight rod or bar; rule; standard of excellence,"

The original manuscripts (literally handwritten) were dictated by the Word (the 'Rock', Christ Jesus) to the Old Testament prophets; and the New Testament manuscripts by the risen Christ to His disciples and apostles, and written down by them under the inspiration of the Holy Spirit.

The Canonised Bible is *the* standard by which all writings, commentaries, histories, archaeological finds, etc., should be judged for accuracy, certainly not the other way around.

2 Timothy 3:15 And that from a child thou hast known the holy scriptures, which are able to make thee wise unto salvation through faith which is in Christ Jesus.

What are the 'holy scriptures' of this verse? Timothy is talking about the Old Testament Canon.

2 Timothy 3:16 All scripture (Strong's 1121gram'-mah; a writing, i.e. a letter, scripture, note, epistle, book, etc.) is given by inspiration of God, and is profitable for doctrine, for reproof, for correction, for instruction in righteousness: 17 That the man of God may be perfect, thoroughly furnished unto all good works.

When it says 'all scripture', the word 'scripture' literally means 'writings'. Clearly all 'writings' are not produced by the inspiration of God. So what does this mean? It means all 'Canonised' writings that were inspired by God, and assembled by Him through the priest Ezra to define and produce the Old Testament; and through Christ's brother John who assembled the New Testament, were exactly as God wanted them to be. Ezra and John were directly inspired by God and Christ to put only those writings that were inspired by God into the Old and New Testament Canons.

The Bible in the form created by God is Perfect like the rest of His Creation.

*Deuteronomy 32:3 Because I will publish the name of the LORD: ascribe ye greatness unto our God. 4 He is the Rock (Christ – 1 Cor 10:4), his work is **perfect**: for all his ways are judgment: a God of truth and without iniquity, just and right is he.*

*Psalm 19:7 The law of the Lord is **perfect**, converting the soul: the testimony of the Lord is sure, making wise the simple.*

The Original Manuscripts of the Bible were assembled by God in a very specific order.

Certainly there is a need for us to be diligent in rooting out the truth from the original texts from time to time, and that Christ through the flow of God's Holy Spirit will help us to do that if we ask in faith. We can rely that with the help of Holy Spirit, we need no man or woman from any human organisation to teach us.

1 John 2:27 But the anointing which ye have received of him abideth in you, and ye need not that any man teach you: but as the same anointing teacheth you of all things, and is truth, and is no lie, and even as it hath taught you, ye shall abide in him.

The thirty thousand different denominations of 'Churchianity' are all human organisations which interpret the Bible to suit their opinions and beliefs. Few of them present the Bible as it should be presented, with awe, respect and honour.

Christ referred to the three sections of the Canon of the Old Testament which was completed by Ezra in the end of the 5th Century B.C. as recorded by Luke.

A fascinating article by Dr. Ernest L. Martin on the Canon of the Old Testament may be found at

http://www.askelm.com/restoring/res006.htm

*Luke 24:44 And he said unto them, These are the words which I spake unto you, while I was yet with you, that all things must be fulfilled, which were written in **the law of Moses**, and in the **prophets**, and in the **psalms**, concerning me.*

The Original Manuscripts, although copied, were absolutely Accurate

When the Prophets, Disciples, and Apostles were expounding points of doctrine, or teaching in parables and symbols, they spoke with authority and conviction and with a feeling of fervour and passion. They were inspired by our Lord, or The Word of the Old Testament, who became Christ Jesus, to write down **accurately** word for word, and teach a message that it was very important for the world to hear and understand.

The original Scriptures of the Old Testament were entrusted to the Jewish Priests, who were meticulous in their care of them. People who question the accuracy of the copies of the ancient manuscripts are probably unaware of the great care that was taken in the process of copying. When scribes were copying manuscripts, each page was carefully checked by men with professional training called "Sopherim' or 'Counters'.

The work of the 'Counter' was to check each letter, and count the number of letters on the page. If there was any mistake, or any difference from the number of words in the original, the whole page was scrapped and the scribe had to write it again.

The New Testament Canon of manuscripts was assembled by Peter and John. It is a list of twenty-seven books 'agreed-upon' by the Apostles that includes the Gospels, Acts, letters of the Apostles and Revelation all written before the end of the 1st century.

Christ's birth was prophesied by Himself in the Old Testament, which He as the Word, the Rock, wrote by inspiration.

Luke 1:67 And his (John the Baptist's) father Zacharias (a righteous priest) was filled with the Holy Ghost, and prophesied, saying, 68 Blessed be the Lord God of Israel; for he hath visited and redeemed his people, 69 And hath raised up an horn of salvation for us in the house of his servant David; 70 As he spake by the mouth of his holy prophets, which have been since the world began:

Also God spoke by Moses in the law.

Acts 3:20 And he shall send Jesus Christ, which before was preached unto you: 21 Whom the heaven must receive until the times of restitution of all things, which God hath spoken by the mouth of all his holy prophets since the world began. 22 For Moses truly said unto the fathers, A prophet shall the Lord your God raise up unto you of your brethren, like unto me; him shall ye hear in all things whatsoever he shall say unto you.

When Christ quoted the Law of Moses, these people were very familiar with the Scriptures, and had learned them from childhood.

Luke 24:24 And certain of them (who had been followers of Christ) which were with us went to the sepulchre, and found it even so as the women had said: but him they saw not. 25 Then he said unto them, O fools, and slow of heart to believe all that the prophets have spoken: 26 Ought not Christ to have suffered these things, and to enter into his glory? 27 And beginning at Moses and all the prophets, he expounded unto them in all the scriptures the things concerning himself.

The risen Christ reminded his disciples about all the prophets had foretold about His coming, but they did not realise it was Him.

Luke 24:28 And they drew nigh unto the village, whither they went: and he made as though he would have gone further. 29 But they constrained him, saying, Abide with us: for it is toward evening, and the day is far spent. And he went in to tarry with them. 30 And it came to pass, as he sat at meat with them, he took bread, and blessed it, and brake, and gave to them. 31 And their eyes were opened, and they knew him; and he vanished out of their sight. 32 And they said one to another, Did not our heart burn within us, while he talked with us by the way, and while he opened to us the scriptures? ...

They suddenly realised that it was indeed the risen Christ.

Luke 24:44 And he said unto them, These are the words which I spake unto you, while I was yet with you, that all things must be fulfilled, which were written in the law of Moses, and in the prophets, and in the psalms, concerning me. 45 Then opened he their understanding, that they might understand the scriptures, 46 And said unto them, Thus it is written, and thus it behooved Christ to suffer, and to rise from the dead the third day: 47 And that repentance and remission of sins should be preached in his name among all nations, beginning at Jerusalem. 48 And ye are witnesses of these things. 49 And, behold, I send the promise of my Father upon you: but tarry ye in the city of Jerusalem, until ye be endued with power from on high. 50 And he led them out as far as to Bethany, and he lifted up his hands, and blessed them. 51 And it came to pass, while he blessed them, he was parted from them, and carried up into heaven.

This was the last time the disciples saw the risen Christ.

The format of the books of the Scriptures was changed in the 1st Century and also later on.

There was a great deal of trouble going on in the 1st Century A.D., with many perverting the Gospel. Paul talked about it in Galatians.

Galatians 1:6 I marvel that ye are so soon removed from him that called you into the grace of Christ unto another gospel: 7 Which is not another; but there be some that trouble you, and would pervert the gospel of Christ.

Then in the 4th Century, 325 A.D., the Catholic church began to make inroads on polluting the purity of the Biblical record, and made many changes in what was presented as Christianity. One of the main changes was the emphasis regarding the state of the dead, and the concept of the immortality of the soul.

The format of the Bible we have today does not consist of the same number of books, nor are they in the same order as the original texts. It is important for us to know this fact, as the current format confuses the story thread of the Bible and completely obscures the original perfect architecture of God's Word.

In the middle of the 4th century a catholic 'Saint', St. Jerome 347-420 A.D., a young scholar at Rome, worked on creating a unified Latin version of the Bible's New Testament. In 386 A.D., Jerome translated sections of the Old Testament from Hebrew into Latin, creating the Roman Catholic Church's *Vulgate*.

Not long after this Jerome, a Catholic priest, translated the Bible and formed it into sixty-six books in a different order from the original texts. Interestingly, six is the number of man! Jerome dispensed with the inspired order of all the original manuscripts, and the result of his work was the basis of the Bible we have now.

The structure and order of God's original manuscripts contains forty-nine (7x7) books, a perfect number. The first five books of the Old Testament, Genesis, Exodus, Leviticus, Deuteronomy, and Numbers comprised 'The Law' of God. The first five books of the New Testament, Matthew, Mark, Luke, John, Acts make up the New Law of Love.

In the original order, these books of Christ's New Law are exactly in the centre of the Bible with twenty-two books of the Old Testament on one side, and the twenty-two books of the New Testament on the other. Christ's birth, life, teaching, death and resurrection, and the giving of Holy Spirit are the exact centre of the Bible. Perfect symmetry!

A copy of this copyright chart may be obtained from :

bhb@ernestworkman.com for study purposes only.

A chart showing this Divine number and order of Books is reproduced on the opposite page:

CHART OF ORIGINAL STRUCTURE OF THE BIBLE

Volume One — The Old Testament

3	Grand	Divisions
The Law — GOD (6 Books)	The Church (1st Rank)	The State (2nd Rank) (11 Books)

1. LAW

1. LAW
1. Genesis
2. Exodus
3. Leviticus
4. Numbers
5. Deuteronomy

[The Old Testament Pentateuch is the beginning two divisions of the Holy Scripture. The Prophets' division in rank is subsidiary to the Law. The Prophets were direct emissaries of God and were responsible for instructing and admonishing rulers and kings. The positioning shows authority of rank and teaching.]

2. PROPHETS

2. FORMER
1. Joshua - Judges
2. Book of the Kingdoms

3. LATTER
3. Isaiah
4. Jeremiah } MAJOR
5. Ezekiel

4. MINOR
6. The Twelve
1. Hosea
2. Joel
3. Amos
4. Obadiah
5. Micah
6. Nahum
7. ...
8. Habakkuk
9. Zephaniah
10. Haggai
11. Zechariah
12. Malachi

(Assyrian Period / Chaldean Period / Restoration Period)

3. PSALMS

5. WISDOM
1. Psalms
2. Proverbs
3. Job

6. FESTIVAL
4. Song = Passover
5. Ruth = Pentecost
6. Lamen. = Ab 10th
7. Eccl. = Tabernacles
8. Esther = Purim

7. RESTORATION
9. Daniel
10. Ezra-Nehemiah
11. Chronicles

[This third division is the Royal (state or government) section and was inferior in rank to the prophets of division two.]

Kings & Rulers + 11 Books = 22 Books

Basic Law 5 Books + Priests & Prophets 6 Books = 11 Books

22 Books — 24 Books

New Testament PENTATEUCH

1 MATT	2 MARK	3 LUKE	4 JOHN	5 ACTS
Jewish	Jewish Gentile	Gentile	Universal	Universal — to Rome?
	PETER	PAUL	JOHN	

4. GOSPELS & ACTS (5 Books)

1. ON EARTH — Gospels (Christ on earth)
2. IN HEAVEN — Acts (Christ in heaven)

22 Books | 22 Books

5 — New Testament Books — PENTATEUCH — "THE FOUNDATION" II Cor. 3:11

5 Books

I. The First Christian Principles — Grade School
(The central historical division of both Testaments)

GOSPELS & ACTS (5) Books
LUKE

49 Books (7 X 7)

Volume Two — The New Testament

3	Grand	Divisions
GOD (1 Book)	The Gentile (2nd Rank) (14 Books)	World Holocaust
	The Jew (1st Rank) (7 Books)	

5. GENERAL

3. UNIVERSAL
1. James
2. I Peter
3. II Peter
4. I John
5. II John
6. III John
7. Jude

[These seven epistles were primarily intended for the Jewish people. Their theme is non-doctrinal and introductory to Paul's doctrinal epistles. They are placed in first position to fulfil the principle "to the Jew first" (Romans 2:10). They are directed to Jewish Christians in general and not to specific churches. They were written by the "pillar" apostles with top rank over Paul.]

6. PAUL

4. 7 CHURCHES
1. Rom.
2. I Cor.
3. II Cor.
4. Gal.   (I. The ABC's of Christian Doctrine)
5. Eph.
6. Phil.
7. Col.   (II. The XYZ's of Doctrine)
8. I Thes.
9. II Thes. (III. The End-Times)

5. MILLENNIAL
10. Hebrews (Temple Symbolism)

6. MINISTERIAL
11. I Tim.
12. II Tim.
13. Titus
14. Phile. (The Epistles for Professional Leaders)

7. REVELATION

7. PROPHETIC
Revelation
The Book of Sevens
1. Seven Churches
2. Seven Golden Candlesticks
3. Seven Stars
4. Seven Spirits of God
5. Seven Lamps of Fire
6. Seven Seals
7. Seven Horns
8. Seven Eyes
9. Seven Angels
10. Seven Trumpets
11. Seven Thunders
12. Seven Thousand Men
13. Seven Heads
14. Seven Crowns
15. Seven Last Plagues
16. Seven Golden Vials
17. Seven Mountains
18. Seven Kings

[The Book of Revelation has all the earmarks of being the final book of both Testaments.]

II. High School
III. College
IV. Post Graduate Studies

22 Books — 24 Books — 22 Books

Designed by Guy K. Arceheau

© 1994 Ernest L. Martin

Translations of the Bible do contain errors.

However, all translations of the original manuscripts are prone to human error, and this should be taken into account whenever we study. Overall, the King James Version is possibly the most reliable translation, which is the reason it has been used for the quotations in this book.

The 1611 King James Version is possibly the finest, largely accurate translation we have. It is written in wonderful stately language and poetic prose. But sadly King James put all kinds of restrictions on the around sixty scholarly translators.

This included ordering and insisting that the Greek word *'ekklesia'* (which means 'group' or assembly') must be the translated into the English word 'Church' which appears one hundred and eleven times in the New Testament. Is the word 'church' a suitable word to use of the 'ecclesia'? Absolutely not!! This was explained in Chapter One.

This is repeated here. Some think that this error does not matter at all, and is irrelevant, but anyone who examines the origin of the word 'church' will find it is based on the mythical goddess 'circe' (*pronounced 'Kirky' – Welsh and Scottish 'Kirk'*) who was a sexual 'nymph', a witch, a sorceress, who used drugs and 'magic' to turn men into animals. Mythical she might be, but this word is totally unsuitable to be used in any connection whatsoever with the *ekklesia, the 'body' of Christ Jesus!!*

The fact that there are some errors of translation need not be a problem as such errors are easily checked by the earnest student. The work of exact translation of the words in the Hebrew, Greek, and other texts has been done by scholars through the ages.

For instance, one reliable source is Strong's Concordance which is available online, although one has to be aware that is does have some religious bias, but that does not in any way preclude it from being a very valuable resource to those who do not know Hebrew or Greek. There are many other resources available to the serious student.

The Dogmatic Teachings of the Bible

The men of God gave no 'perhaps', no possibilities or 'maybe's' when they were speaking. There are ways we can present teachings without doing it in such a manner as to give offence. Being 'dogmatic' is not always a good idea, as it tends to bespeak arrogance, which is not the Christian way.

However, there are things that the Bible is dogmatic about, and that we should be 'dogmatic' about too. For instance:

We can affirm with assurance that we believe that true Christianity, when based carefully on the teachings of the original manuscripts upon which the Bible is based, which is God's Word to us His children, is an absolute. We can be dogmatic about that, and hopefully every Christian would be able to be as well.

 One could also state that we do not believe that Buddhism, Taoism, Confucianism, Islam, Baha'i, or Shinto doctrines were religions spread into the world by the inspiration of God, although one might have to be cautious and respectful if expressing that to others.

It is imperative that true Christians cultivate an attitude of total trust and belief that the Bible is accurate, and indeed is God talking to us here and now. That is right, the actual Almighty God and His Son Jesus Christ who created all things, designed this Book to tell us about Their Plan for Humankind.

Ask for God's help, pray for Him to cause His Holy Spirit to flow into your mind so that you can really get excited about it!

*Hebrews 11:6 But without faith it is **impossible** to please him: for he that cometh to God must believe that he is, and that he is a rewarder of them that diligently seek him.*

Anyone who dedicates time and effort into their study of the Scriptures for knowledge, understanding and wisdom concerning God's Purpose and His Plan will be rewarded beyond belief.

Philippians 4:7 And the peace of God, which passeth all understanding, shall keep your hearts and minds through Christ Jesus.

The next chapter offers some helpful tools which may be used to enable effective study of the Bible.

CHAPTER 5

HOW TO STUDY GOD'S WORD EFFECTIVELY

After spending most of my adult life spending time reading and studying the Bible, I thought I knew the Book fairly well. Then when I read the 'keys' to understanding the Bible better suggested by Dr. Ernest L. Martin at age seventy-eight, and started to use them, my appreciation of God's Word quickly expanded at an exponential rate.

An important reason for our proper and careful study of God's Word using the 'keys' offered here, is to be able to 'rightly divide' and make partitions between the truth and the error in the doctrines we have been taught, and have believed in our previous or current experiences with 'Churchianity'.

Here are the simple yet profound 'keys' he recommended using to unlock the meaning of the Scriptures:

Key #1. First ask God for the help of Holy Spirit every time we study.
The very fact that we have an earnest desire to study the Word of God means that God has given us that inclination, and the wish to learn more about Him. A wonderful gift.

Romans 1:6 For to be carnally minded is death; but to be spiritually minded is life and peace.

So we can rejoice at this thought that every time we approach the Bible we can know that we have the help of God's Spirit to make our minds compliant.

*Matthew 13:15 For this people's heart is waxed gross, and their ears are dull of hearing, and **their eyes they have closed**; lest at any time they should see with their eyes and hear with their ears, and should understand with their heart, and should be converted, and I should heal them.*

This applies to the average churchgoer! Our human carnal minds actually resist God without realising it. He tells us that anyone whose mind has not been opened is against God, not for Him. The average person in this world has their 'eyes shut' and 'ears closed' when it comes to knowing God in Truth.

So it is vital for us to ask for the Spiritual gifts that are needed to progress in the search for knowledge, understanding, and wisdom. Here is an example of these three.

Knowledge is the 'knowing' that you have electricity in your home and when you operate a switch, the light comes on.

Proverbs 18:15 The heart of the prudent getteth knowledge; and the ear of the wise seeketh knowledge.

Understanding is the understanding that there is a power station in your locality, and that there are wires from there that connect your house to the electricity supply.

Proverbs 1:5 A wise man will hear, and will increase learning; and a man of understanding shall attain unto wise counsels:

Wisdom is to know when and whether to turn the light on or off.

Proverbs 4:7 Wisdom is the principal thing; therefore get wisdom:

James 1:5 If any of you lack wisdom, let him ask of God, that giveth to all men liberally, and upbraideth not; and it shall be given him.

Proverbs 2:1 My son, if thou wilt receive my words, and hide my commandments with thee; 2 So that thou incline thine ear unto wisdom, and apply thine heart to understanding; 3 Yea, if thou criest after knowledge, and liftest up thy voice for understanding;

We also need to ask for the spiritual gifts of belief, faith, humility, penitence, repentance, open mindedness, and teachableness.

Key #2. God has written His Book in His Structure, Language & Styles

God's language is not our language. His way of thinking is not our way.

Isaiah 55:8 For my thoughts are not your thoughts, neither are your ways my ways, saith the LORD. 9 For as the heavens are higher than the earth, so are my ways higher than your ways, and my thoughts than your thoughts.

So His Book is not like any other Book. It is written in His Style, His thoughts, His Language. However, we can be on His 'wavelength', and 'on the same page' with Him so to speak if we ask for His help.

Structure

God put His Book together through centuries of time, and through many different people, a miracle in itself! The Bible is about His Plan for the production and development of His human children whose destiny is to become part of God's

Family of Spirit Beings. The story starts simply, and gradually builds up the details of His Plan all through the Book.

One way to describe this structure is 'Progressive Revelation'. As we progress through the Book, we will appreciate that the story is delivered in 'bite size' chunks. Or as quoted previously and explained in chapter 4, the manner of the 'structure' of the Book is illustrated in the book of Isaiah.

Isaiah 28:10 For precept must be upon precept, precept upon precept; line upon line, line upon line; here a little, and there a little: 11 For with stammering lips and another tongue will he speak to this people.

Regrettably many religious ministers misuse the knowledge of this principle. They take verses of the Bible 'here and there' to 'prove' their point, or to persuade people to their way of thinking. That is how the thousands of denominations came about. Everyone thinks they are right.

Proverbs 21:2 Every way of a man is right in his own eyes: but the LORD pondereth the hearts.

This book is written with that principle in mind. As far as it is possible, personal opinions are avoided. The writer is helped what to think by carefully examining and dividing God's Word of Truth while seeking His guidance.

Jeremiah 10:23 O LORD, I know that the way of man is not in himself: it is not in man that walketh to direct his steps.

No, human beings do not know how to 'direct' their steps in the manner that God wants them to. Just look at the state of the world!

Regarding structure, it is well for us to know that the chapter divisions and verse numbering in our English Bibles were not part of the original texts. They were put in by well meaning people to make navigation of the Scriptures easier, and they do. However, being aware that they are not necessarily 'inspired' can help us to determine the true meaning of what we are reading.

Language

The original manuscripts were dictated personally by Christ Jesus to His servants and were in Hebrew, Greek and Aramaic. Hebrew is unique in the complexity of its meanings of words. It can be very direct, and also very poetic. Greek is different, and there we have the advantage a large proportion of the English language being derived from Greek words.

However, it is wise to check the meanings of words, and this has been made possible by the scholars of each of the three languages. So in our studies, especially of verses with which we feel we are most familiar it is good to check important words for clarity. If we decide to look up the definition of the specific meaning of every significant word, often the 'lights come on' and we get to see depths of meaning we may have missed in that verse all our lives.

Strong's Concordance is very useful in this regard, and is available free to download on the internet. Of course like any other work of men external to the Bible, it may have bias on certain topics. The same is true of commentaries and other Bible helps, but so long as we check as we go along that what they say harmonises with the Truths of the Bible, they can be of great help.

Styles

People who do not realise the Bible is written in many different 'styles' can get into a real muddle. If the reader takes symbolic or figurative statements literally, and vice versa, conflict, confusion, and apparent contradictions leap out of the page! There are many styles.

Literal Statements Much of the Bible contains information that needs to be taken literally.

Symbols in the Bible are very important, and need to be recognised as such, as they point to a truth or truths, and we need to heed the underlying meaning of them. Avoid taking them literally.

Figures of speech abound in the Bible, and should never be taken literally. If one says, "I am dying for a coffee" in English, nobody takes that literally! The same is true with 'figurative' statements in the Bible. Take them for what they are. God often uses 'figures' to illustrate important facts and make them more clear.

Poetic language also appears frequently in the Bible. Poetry can often get a point, or a feeling, or a thought across in a most powerful way. But nobody would think that "I wandered lonely as a cloud, that floats on high over vale and hill" was literal, but the beauty of Wordsworth's most famous poem lives on over two hundred years since it was written in 1804.

Parables are stories to illustrate a point, and to get a deeper meaning across. If we realise this, we will get more out of them.

Punctuation is important. The punctuation in the Bible does not always help clarity. Here is a humourous example in English where a comma in the wrong place makes the meaning totally different. This is not in the Bible!

Caesar entered on his head, his helmet in his hand, his trusty sword...

Caesar entered, on his head his helmet, in his hand his trusty sword...

So when reading, if the punctuation interferes with meaning, perhaps you might check other translations.

Conversation and Narrative The Book of Job is the oldest book of the Bible. It is almost all conversation and narrative. First it is between Job and men, then later between God and Job, and finally between Job and God. In places it is factual, in others it is poetic, and in others God reveals Himself in His great Power.

The entire Bible is rich in many forms and styles, be clear about which style or device is being used in any passage, and let those styles 'talk' to you. If we go with the flow, and allow our minds to bathe in God's Word, we will be spiritually and even physically nourished.

Matthew 4:4 But he answered and said, It is written, Man shall not live by bread alone, but by every word that proceedeth out of the mouth of God.

Key #3. Use a reliable translation, the King James is good but has errors.

All translations contain errors, but don't let that put you off!

Just always be alert for the need to check the original manuscripts if ever in doubt about the meaning of any verse or passage. Check each word or phrase in the Hebrew, Greek or Aramaic using the appropriate resource.

Other modern translations might help clarity, but be cautious as many of them will contain doctrinal bias. Just be on your guard and ask for guidance from Above.

Key #4. Be sure to check the context when looking at any verse or passage.

Being careful to take into account the context of any passage is possibly the most important key to correct understanding of any Scripture.

A great deal of misunderstanding of the Scriptures does occur when single verses or passages are taken out of context. A lot of the doctrines of the churches of this world rely on the interpretation of verses or passages taken out of context by the church hierarchy and ministry.

Here is an example. Some Church organisations teach that 'tithing' is required of a Christian. This is not true. In fact the Bible teaches that it would be a sin to ask anyone for tithes, or indeed for them to pay tithes in this era! Here is a verse that they quote, to imply that the Christian is 'robbing God' if they do not faithfully pay their tithes.

*Malachi 3:8 **Will a man rob God?** Yet ye have robbed me. But ye say, Wherein have we robbed thee? In tithes and offerings.*

That looks pretty clear, does it not? Yes it does, but when we look into the context, we will find that it is not talking to Christians today at all. It is well to remember the principle that the Bible interprets the Bible.

The Jews, to whom this verse was addressed had been released from captivity, and were commanded to return to Israel and rebuild the Temple which had been destroyed seventy years previously. They had been back in the land of Israel for nineteen years, and still had not begun work on the Temple. So God was not happy with them!

The prophet Haggai gives some crucial information about the situation.

Haggai 1:2 Thus speaketh the LORD of hosts, saying, This people say, The time is not come, the time that the LORD's house should be built. 3 Then came the word of the LORD by Haggai the prophet, saying, 4 Is it time for you, O ye, to dwell in your cieled houses, and this house lie waste? 5 Now therefore thus saith the LORD of hosts; Consider your ways.

The Jews had found time to build themselves quality houses with nice ceilings, and establish their own businesses, but in 19 years had not started on God's house! Furthermore, the Jews were complaining bitterly that God had not blessed their crops, and had sent them bad weather to punish them because God's house still lay waste.

Haggai 1:8 Go up to the mountain, and bring wood, and build the house; and I will take pleasure in it, and I will be glorified, saith the LORD. 9 Ye looked for much, and, lo it came to little; and when ye brought it home, I did blow upon it. Why? saith the LORD of hosts. Because of mine house that is waste, and ye run every man unto his own house.

But they still ignored the Prophet's words. Even though God had warned the Jews twice to 'consider' their wayward ways, they had not. So when we look at Malachi 3:8 in the context of the story of the time, the Prophet was reporting for God, telling the Jews that they were robbing God by spending money on their own homes, and not giving tithes for the building of God's house.

To be sure we understand that this only applied to them back then, and not to us today, here are a couple of facts. When the tithing system had been established, only the Levitical Priesthood were authorised to collect tithes of farm animals and produce, not money. The tithes were for the upkeep of the Temple and its staff. There is no Levitical Priesthood today, and no Temple so the tithing system passed into history, and no longer can apply.

This does not stop denominations of 'Churchianity' from asking for tithes, or putting their adherents under pressure with emotional and spiritual blackmail to support their churches financially. Some organisations have become very, very rich indeed in this way. God says that they false prophets making merchandise of their followers.

2 Peter 2:1 But there were false prophets also among the people, even as there shall be false teachers among you, who privily shall bring in damnable heresies, even denying the Lord that bought them, and bring upon themselves swift destruction. 2 And many shall follow their pernicious ways; by reason of whom the way of truth shall be evil spoken of. 3 And through covetousness shall they with feigned words make merchandise of you: whose judgment now of a long time lingereth not, and their damnation slumbereth not.

There was at least one church organisation in the 20th century, which quoted the verse in Malachi 3:8 completely out of context, to demand tithes from its followers, to the extent of hundreds of millions of dollars. In their greed, they insisted members paid a tithe, or tenth, in cash of their earnings, and of the gross salary, not after tax! Not content with that, in their covetousness, they invented a second and third tithe that was totally unbiblical. Religious mafiosi or what!

Key #5 Check the grammatical syntax, and check problematic words in the original texts.
Look out for words like who, what, where, when, why, as these interrogative words sometimes reveal more meaning when examined. When there are any words which are not immediately known or clearly understood, a dictionary, or an etymological dictionary which shows the origination and derivation of words is most useful. Dictionaries of both types are available to refer to free on the Internet.

One key to effective learning any subject is to adopt and practice 'The Dictionary Habit'. Through life, we learn a lot of words by hearing them in a certain context which reveals their meaning to a degree. We might find it difficult to define or explain the derivation of many words that we might be familiar with. Adopting the habit of checking with dictionaries, particularly etymological dictionaries, leads to expansion of the mind, and increased understanding. Intelligence, or the ability to learn, is enhanced as our vocabulary grows.

Key #6. Note the timing or chronology of the event.

Chronological indications can be very important, especially because when we rightly divide the Scriptures, many are relevant for one time and not another. In other cases, the knowledge, understanding and wisdom is relevant for all time.

A habit of noticing words like, before, after, now, when, then, days, years, in the reign of, and so on will help one to be aware of indications of a time frame that could well be significant.

For instance, the Laws of the Old Testament were specifically designed for the people at the time. Early on in the Law, the statutes were for a people who were itinerant. Later on, they were more specific to people who lived in one place.

Also, once Christ came and fulfilled the Law for us, many of the physical aspects of the Law passed into history or became spiritual. Examples are the sacrificial system, the Holy Days, and circumcision which are no longer to be observed physically, but most certainly have spiritual relevance for us today.

Key #7 Then take account of the geography where relevant.

Most Bibles have a section at the back with maps, and lists of places. It is sometimes helpful to have an idea of the geographical area where what we are reading took place. The habit of noticing place names can be useful, and checking their location on a map to get a better picture of events.

Key #8 Navigating the Scriptures, finding words, verses, subjects etc

There is an amazing, and incredibly fast way to find anything you are looking for in the Bible. People have done all the work of putting the entire words of the Bible in many versions and translations onto databases. These are indexed in such a way, as to make accessing anything instant.

The one this author uses all the time, many times a day, is to be found at:

https://www.biblegateway.com

It is free to use, so long as you do not mind the adverts which are easy enough to ignore. There are many others, but this is the one I found easy to use.

Key #9 Set up a special working area, with all the necessary tools.

Pens, pencils, notebooks, a good reading light, a special reading frame so that you can put your Bible at a good reading angle. Use a comfortable chair. And surround yourself with anything else you feel would make your area conducive to workmanlike study.

Key #10 For your health's sake, discipline yourself to get up and move around at regular intervals.

A mini-trampoline is a valuable health aid. It is the most beneficial exercise aid to help circulation of blood and lymph, and keeps your muscles in tone.

Just a couple of minutes of gentle movements on it every hour or less, are really worth the time spent. It will clear your head, re-energise your body, and clear your mind. This suggestion comes from much experience! Enjoy!

Author's note: These wonderful tools or 'keys' have enabled me to study in a much more in-depth, knowledgeable, and workmanlike manner than I ever did for so many decades on my own

Postscript.

For those who might be interested, one of Dr. Martin's passions before he died in 2002 was to see a new perfect translation of the original texts in the correct order, in lovely clear language, and felt is was not only very desirable but definitely possible. He had started work on it but it was never completed.

Another Bible produced in 2009 is a 'literal' translation which as far as it is possible, avoids colouring the text with religious opinion. It is called 'The Hebraic Roots Bible' It is published by Congregation of YHWH, Jerusalem, PO Box 832, Carteret, New Jersey, U.S.A. It is available from Amazon.

HOW TO STUDY GOD'S WORD EFFECTIVELY

CHAPTER 6

Christian Works and Their Reward

SALVATION IS A FREE GIFT FROM GOD TO ALL

For by grace are ye saved through faith; and that not of yourselves: it is the gift of God: Not of works, lest any man should boast. For we are his workmanship, created in Christ Jesus unto good works, which God hath before ordained that we should walk in them.
Ephesians 2:8-10

Yes, we are saved by Grace, and there is nothing we have to do to earn it, as it is a gift. However, there are positive things we can do in our Christian lives to qualify for the first resurrection. We are created in Christ to do good works, and 'walk' in them day by day. God wants us to choose His way of life.

The first Commandment is our powerful foundation for our 'works':

*Deuteronomy 6:5 And **thou shalt love** the Lord thy God with all thine heart, and with all thy soul, and with all thy might.*

Practical ways to show our love of God to God
We human beings are made in God's image, and our destiny is to become His children. What are practical ways we can

love God? The Bible teaches us a basic practical way is to keep His Wishes and Commands. Jesus said:

John 14:15 If ye love me, keep my commandments.

Christ's commandments are **not** the same as the Ten Commandments. Some denominations in 'Churchianity' insist that Christ is referring here to the 'Ten', but He is most certainly not. This will be made clear a little later when consideration is given to what Christ said in the 'Sermon on the Mount'.

The same instruction applies to one way we are to love God our Father.

1 John 5:3 For this is the love of God, that we keep his commandments: and his commandments are not grievous.

Because we are made in God's image, and God is Love, we are capable as humans to think about love, and practice being loving.

1 John 4:8 He that loveth not knoweth not God; for God is love.

Friends, we know how we like to be loved by our fellow human beings. Here are some major ways we like to be treated and loved by others.

As human beings, we like to:

Be loved for who we are.

Be trusted and respected.

Be appreciated, and thanked.

Be considered.

Spend time with those who love us.

Keep in touch with those who love us.

Have those who love us to be kind, merciful and forgiving to us.

Have our work to be admired and praised.

So how can we love God in down to earth, simple ways?

Because we are made in God's image, when we are in contact with Him, and our carnal human nature is kept in check because His Holy Spirit is flowing in our minds; we like the same things God likes.

So from this we can know how to love God in practical ways.

God likes to be loved for Who and What He is.

He wants to be respected trusted, thanked and considered.

He likes His work of Creation to be admired and praised.

He wants His amazing, breathtaking, wonderful Plan for us to be appreciated.

He likes and wants His ecclesia to spend time with Him and with His Word

He wants us to keep in touch with Him through prayer.

God wants us to acknowledge his kindness, mercy and forgiveness to us.

God wants us to LOVE HIM by keeping His commandments!

We can have this constant attitude of mind and spirit if we ask Him for it.

The love chapter in the Bible is 1 Corinthians 13.

When asked to read this chapter in a service at age twelve, I memorised it, and that has been a wonderful source of meaning about love to refer to in my mind ever since.

To make this chapter easier to read in the KJV, and to get the most out of it, it is a good idea to replace the old English word 'charity' with the word 'love' as you read it. These verses light up and expand our understanding of the one word 'LOVE' which has so many facets of deep meaning.

Here is the chapter in the 'Good News' translation, which is less majestic, but in clear more modern English.

I may be able to speak the languages of human beings and even of angels, but if I have no love, my speech is no more than a noisy gong or a clanging bell. 2 I may have the gift of inspired preaching; I may have all knowledge and understand all secrets; I may have all the faith needed to move mountains—but if I have no love, I am nothing. 3 I may give away everything I have, and even give up my body to be burned but if I have no love, this does me no good. 4 Love is patient and kind; it is not jealous or conceited or proud; 5 love is not ill-mannered or selfish or irritable; love does not keep a record of wrongs; 6 love is not happy with evil, but is happy with the truth. 7 Love never gives up; and its faith, hope, and patience never fail. 8 Love is eternal. There are inspired messages, but they are temporary; there are gifts of speaking in strange tongues, but they will cease; there is knowledge, but it will pass. 9 For our gifts of knowledge and of inspired messages are only partial; 10 but when what is perfect comes, then what is partial will disappear. 11 When I was a child, my speech, feelings, and thinking were all those of a child; now that I am an adult, I have no more use for childish ways. 12 What we see now is like a dim image in a mirror; then we shall see face-to-face. What I know now is only partial; then it will be complete - as complete as God's knowledge of me. 13 Meanwhile these three remain: faith, hope, and love; and the greatest of these is love.

WORKS ARE THE CHRISTIAN WAY OF LIFE

Deuteronomy 30:19 I call heaven and earth to record this day against you, that I have set before you life and death, blessing and cursing: therefore choose life, that both thou and thy seed may live: 20 That thou mayest love the LORD thy God, and that thou mayest obey his voice, and that thou mayest cleave unto him: for he is thy life, and the length of thy days:

God works. We are made in the image and likeness of God. And so we should work too.

John 5:17 But Jesus answered them, My Father worketh hitherto, and I work.

Christ the man also makes it clear that it was not He who was doing the work of the Father, but it was the Father who was doing the work through Him.

John 14:10 Believest thou not that I am in the Father, and the Father in me? the words that I speak unto you I speak not of myself: but the Father that dwelleth in me, he doeth the works.

This is also true of the 'works' we do as Christians. All the 'works' we do is to be done by God working in and through us.

If we attempt to run our own lives without God working through us, we risk doing our own works rather than the works God would have us do.

BEWARE FALSE 'GOSPELS' – RELIGIOUS OR SECULAR

There are many EGO-driven counterfeit alluring man-made 'gospels' competing for our attention in this world.

Galatians 1:6 I marvel that ye are so soon removed from him that called you into the grace of Christ unto another gospel: 7 Which is not another; but there be some that trouble you, and would pervert the gospel of Christ.

Christ taught His disciples that the true Gospel has two main thrusts:

Luke 9:2 And he sent them to preach the kingdom of God, and to heal the sick.

That is part of the work of a Christian to this day. That does not mean we should necessarily go out and 'beat the bushes' for people to listen, or to be preachy to others. The 'status quo' is that God is in charge of whose minds He opens now, and the vast majority whose minds are blinded at this time. It is not a Christian's work to push against the Will of God in any regard, the very opposite, 'Thy Will be done, O lord!'

However, it does mean that we need to be living examples of what it means to be a true Christian; in good health, and clearly full of the joy of the knowledge of our future in the Kingdom of God that we are working towards.

There is some thought that good health is only attained by severely restricting what they eat. Some people become vegetarians, others strive even harder to become vegans. Interesting that Christ ate meat and fish, grains, and took His people into a land of 'milk and honey', and drank wine. His first miracle was to make a large quantity from water at a wedding feast.

Total abstainers suggest that Christ made grape juice, but the Bible records that He was called a 'wine bibber' so that is unlikely! Others were not happy with John the Baptist because he ate locusts and wild honey.

Matthew 11:18 For John came neither eating nor drinking, and they say, He hath a devil.19 The Son of man came eating and drinking, and they say, Behold a man gluttonous, and a winebibber, a friend of publicans and sinners. But wisdom is justified of her children.

Clearly in Christ's time, it was not possible to please everyone!

Is our Elder Brother not our example in all aspects of our lives including eating and drinking?

Romans 14:2 For one believeth that he may eat all things: another, who is weak, eateth herbs. 3 Let not him that eateth despise him that eateth not; and let not him which eateth not judge him that eateth: for God hath received him.

The Christian way is not to criticise others regarding what they 'should' or 'should not' eat, or to lay 'burdens' of any sort on others as did the Pharisees. If we are to help others attain and maintain health, let us do that with love and compassion, and never help others to feel badly of themselves.

If the opportunity to 'preach' the Gospel of the Kingdom to anyone who asks us about our faith, wonderful, then we can share our confidence and perhaps even point them in the right direction so that they can 'discover' the truth for themselves if God so Wills.

False 'gospels' preach the 'commandments of men' and leave God out. These are based on the human EGO (which some say stands for '**E**dge**G**od**O**ut!)

Examples of such false 'gospels' are to be found in the teachings of the many "Self-Improvement" gurus. What most of them teach is that we can do all the work of running our lives, with their help of course, and following their 'laws of success'.

Some gurus use as a basis for their teachings a book that has the intriguing title of 'The Secret' which has attracted a large following of enthusiastic true believers.

Some successful teachers offer a way to success that offers many 'laws' which when put into effect by our own energies will produce a superabundance of everything we could ever want in terms of health, happiness, and wealth and all its trappings (interesting word!).

The Law of Supply – this is where you'll learn the truth that there are no limits except the ones which we create ourselves, that you live in a world of abundance where you can have, do and be anything you truly desire.

This law says there are no limits, so long as you do not create them yourself! With this 'tool' you can have do or be anything you want. It is all about the 'me' and what appears to be what used to be called the 'get' way. It appeals to the lower notes of human nature.

The Law of Sacrifice – this often misunderstood law includes the process of harnessing our powers toward a desired end. Giving up something of a lower nature to receive something of a higher nature.

So the purpose of 'sacrifice' is to give something up in order to 'get' something better?? This appears to feed the human tendency for the greedy acquisition of material things. There seems to be little room for the great real sacrifices that some people make for the general good, or to benefit worthy causes without any motive other than love.

The Law of Attraction – this takes you on from The Secret, and into the practical application of Desire, Expectation and Achievement, and also to continually grow – through constant expansion and fuller expression of your true potential.

Many claim that this 'Law of Attraction' works for 90% of those who apply it. Some observers say that has not been true of the many hapless people that have become ensnared in human ego-driven 'get, get, get' ideas, and who continue in straightened circumstances if not worse.

It is also true that many very successful people claim that implementing the laws of these concepts is the 'secret' of their success. That may be true, and it may not be true. Perhaps they were very talented people who knew how to make their way in the world by 'working the system' that some are privy to. God says:

Jeremiah 10:23 O LORD, I know that the way of man is not in himself: it is not in man that walketh to direct his steps.

Proverbs 21:2 Every way of a man is right in his own eyes: but the Lord pondereth the hearts.

What is true is that if we rely on ourselves and the teachings of men in our journey to achieve success in life, and leave God out of the picture, we are in grave danger of making a 'god' out of a human system, and worshipping it, which is idolatry.

Christ finished his commission and work
Christ worked right up to the end, and finished the work the Father had given Him. We should have the 'work' in mind that God has given us to do each day, and think about it like Christ did.

John 17:4 I have glorified thee on the earth: I have finished the work which thou gavest me to do. 5 And now, O Father, glorify thou me with thine own self with the glory which I had with thee before the world was.

Let Christ's mind be in you, and what does that mean in practical terms?

Philippians 2:5 Let this mind be in you, which was also in Christ Jesus:

The word 'mind' in Greek is Strong's (5426) frone>w, — fron-e to exercise the mind, by implication to be (mentally) disposed (more or less earnestly in a certain direction); intensive to interest oneself in (with concern or obedience): — set the affection on, (be) care (-ful), (be like-, + be of one, of the same, + let this) mind (-ed), regard, savour, think.

When it says in verse 5 'let this mind be in you', what exactly does that mean? The previous verse tells us what kind of mind we need to cultivate.

Philippians 2:4 Look not every man on his own things, but every man also on the things of others.

In effect Christ is saying through Paul, 'don't spend all your time thinking about yourself and your life, but focus *also* on the needs of others'. An important part of the 'works' of a Christian is to have a continual desire to be of help and assistance to others. Even in simple matters like being courteous, giving directions, opening doors for others, assisting someone with a heavy bag, and in every and any way we are able to, always within our means and capacity.

Recognise that most of us feel bit lonely at times. It is said that most people can count their true friends on the fingers of one hand. Being a good friend is one 'work' of a Christian. Most friendships seem to be starved of contact because everyone is too 'busy' with their own lives to share time. Keep in touch, a phone call, a card, a visit, give something of yourself to those you care about. This is a way to love them, and God!

So when Paul says in verse 5 let this mind be in you which was also in Christ Jesus, he is talking about the way Christ was and is constantly thinking about the needs of others. This is the type of mind we need to 'let', allow, cultivate and earnestly work on.

Of course we need to think about ourselves, and have loving consideration for our own lives, and at the same time not lose sight of our responsibilities as a Christian to think and care about others in measure.

We do not work out our own Salvation – God does that work.

'Churchianity' ministers often quote this verse...

Philippians 2:12 Wherefore, my beloved, as ye have always obeyed, not as in my presence only, but now much more in my absence, work out your own salvation with fear and trembling.

They mislead their hearers because they do not complete the thought Paul was making in the next verse.

Philippians 2:13 For it is God which worketh in you both to will and to do of his good pleasure.

We do not have to work out our own salvation; that is a Gift of Grace. However, it is not we ourselves who do the daily 'works' of being a Christian, it is God who is working through us to perform His will.

1 Thessalonians 2:13 For this cause also thank we God without ceasing, because, when ye received the word of God which ye heard of us, ye received it not as the word of men, but as it is in truth, the word of God, which effectually worketh also in you that believe.

As we study God's Word, He works with all those that believe giving us gifts of Spiritual insights.

Ephesians 2:10 For we are his workmanship, created in Christ Jesus unto good works, which God hath before ordained that we should walk in them.

Every Christian is 'ordained' by God to do 'good works'.
The word 'ordained' means that as Christians, we are appointed to the service of Christ's ecclesia, the 'body of Christ', and His ministry to do good works.

God encourages us to do good works with His help, so that He can reward us with entry into the Kingdom of God and to a position commensurate with the quality of our work.

1 Corinthians 3:7 So then neither is he that planteth any thing, neither he that watereth; but God that giveth the increase. 8 Now he that planteth and he that watereth are one: and every man shall receive his own reward according to his own labour. 9 For we are labourers together with God: ye are God's husbandry, ye are God's building.

We are part of God's building, our bodies are a Temple.
1 Corinthians 3:16 Know ye not that ye are the temple of God, and that the Spirit of God dwelleth in you? 17 If any man defile the temple of God, him shall God destroy; for the temple of God is holy, which temple ye are.

Strive to be healthy. This is part of the 'work' of a Christian. With our 'Christlike' mind in us, we might also be able to encourage others who ask for our help, to be more health conscious. It is never a good idea to advise or interfere in any way unless asked, and even then proceed with care.

Currently there is a sad epidemic in the western world – obesity from gluttony.

Philippians 3:19 Whose end is destruction, whose God is their belly, and whose glory is in their shame, who mind earthly things.)

The modern diet of manufactured and convenience foods, coupled with a lack of moderate exercise, results in a disastrous state of poor health for millions. Vast numbers are overweight, fat and obese to the degree that many carry around twice their ideal weight. The result of that is mushrooming increase of heart disease, diabetes leading to amputations, and other physical and mental health problems. Such people are becoming an increasingly costly burden on society, and on the 'health' systems that countries are now realising that they can no longer afford.

The solution is actually simple, but it is very difficult for millions to change their habits. We can avoid manufactured and convenience foods like the plague that they are. We can buy natural food that will go bad, and eat it before it does. We can build our health with moderate exercise, just a few minutes a day makes everyone feel better.

When we perform Christian 'works', we are working with God. We are God's 'husbandry', involved with the management of the household of God. We are part of God's business.

Ephesians 2:19 Now therefore ye are no more strangers and foreigners, but fellowcitizens with the saints, and of the household of God;

We are part of His household, and we have our own Temple to take care of, nourish and keep healthy, as well as being a resource for others who are looking to improve their health and well-being.

2 Thessalonians 2:16 Now our Lord Jesus Christ himself, and God, even our Father, which hath loved us, and hath given us everlasting consolation and good hope through grace, 17 Comfort your hearts, and stablish you in every good word and work.

Many people are going to be surprised to find that despite their fervent religious activities, they missed out on being with Christ in the Millennium

Matthew 7:21 Not every one that saith unto me, Lord, Lord, shall enter into the kingdom of heaven; but he that doeth the will of my Father which is in heaven.

What is the reward that Christ will bring with Him?
Christ is coming to establish **the Kingdom of God** with His saints. This Christ said should be our focus in life:

*Matthew 6:33 But seek ye **first** the kingdom of God, and his righteousness; and all these things shall be added unto you.*

What things was Christ talking about? In the few preceding verses He was telling us that He feeds and clothes His Creation. He tells us not to worry about these things as they will be taken care of, so long as we have faith.

Matthew 6:34 Take therefore no (anxious) thought for the morrow: for the morrow shall take thought for the things of itself. Sufficient unto the day is the evil thereof.

Of course we need to be diligent to do our part to take care of ourselves properly in the matters of day to day living, and to trust with faith that He will supply all our needs. Not wants by the way!

Philippians 4:19 But my God shall supply all your need according to his riches in glory by Christ Jesus.

This does not mean that no Christian will ever lack for any real needs like food and clothing. We may at times go through hardships, and that is true.

Revelation 22:12 And, behold, I come quickly; and my reward is with me, to give every man according as his work shall be.

So the reward that Christ will bring with him for His saints is to be installed in the Kingdom of God and to reign with Him.

Matthew 16:27 For the Son of man shall come in the glory of his Father with his angels; and then he shall reward every man according to his works.

Our reward is measured out to each of us individually by Him, and that reward will be proportionate to our diligence in respect of our Christian 'works'

Matthew 25:21 His lord said unto him, Well done, thou good and faithful servant: thou hast been faithful over a few things, I will make thee ruler over many things: enter thou into the joy of thy lord.

This shows that our position in the Kingdom of God is contingent upon the measure of our good works.

Luke 19:17 And he said unto him, Well, thou good servant: because thou hast been faithful in a very little, have thou authority over ten cities.

Those who do less with the talents God gave them will be given less responsibility, perhaps over five cities, or even only one. But that still will be an incredible opportunity to develop as a Brother of Christ! Those who do little or 'bury' their talents, will suffer loss.

Romans 2:10 But glory, honour, and peace, to every man that worketh good, to the Jew first, and also to the Gentile: 11 For there is no respect of persons with God.

God is not a respecter of persons, but He is a respecter of quality work.

Matthew 6:19 Lay not up for yourselves treasures upon earth, where moth and rust doth corrupt, and where thieves break through and steal: 20 But lay up for yourselves treasures in heaven, where neither moth nor rust doth corrupt, and where thieves do not break through nor steal:

What are the treasures in heaven? They are the spiritual gifts we are given to work with belief, faith, repentance, flow of Holy Spirit, knowledge, understanding, wisdom.

Ephesians 4:7 But unto every one of us is given grace according to the measure of the gift of Christ. 8 Wherefore he saith, When he ascended up on high, he led captivity captive, and gave gifts unto men.

God gives us the Spiritual 'tools' to work with and He will not change His mind.

Romans 11:29 For the gifts and calling of God are without repentance.

God's different gifts are all by the same Spirit, His Power in us.

1 Corinthians 12:7 But the manifestation of the Spirit is given to every man to profit withal. 8 For to one is given by the Spirit the word of wisdom; to another the word of knowledge by the same Spirit; 9 To another faith by the same Spirit; to another the gifts of healing by the same Spirit;

God has determined before the world began how He will distribute His gifts to each of His children.

Romans 4:4 Now to him that worketh is the reward not reckoned of grace, but of debt

As we lay up for ourselves 'treasures in heaven', God sets up our treasure as a 'debt' which merits a reward which He will bring with Him at His second coming.

2 Corinthians 9:15 Thanks be unto God for his unspeakable gift.

Give thanks daily for the gift of His Word, His Spirit, His understanding, and His Grace.

What are the Spiritual Works we are to be 'walking' in?

Part of our daily 'work' as a Christian is to make good use of the gifts of the Spirit we have received.

1 Thessalonians 1:2 We give thanks to God always for you all, making mention of you in our prayers; 3 Remembering without ceasing your work of faith, and labour of love, and patience of hope in our Lord Jesus Christ, in the sight of God and our Father;

Faith: Works of faith, love, patience, and hope, increase with use. It is important to ask God for Faith.

James 2:17 Even so faith, if it hath not works, is dead, being alone. 18 Yea, a man may say, Thou hast faith, and I have works: shew me thy faith without thy works, and I will shew thee my faith by my works.

Faith is an essential ingredient of our daily application of ourselves to 'works'. The 'faith' chapter in the Bible is Hebrews 11 which rewards the one who studies it carefully.

Hebrews 11:1 Now **faith is the substance** of things hoped for, **the evidence** of things not seen. 2 For by it the elders obtained a good report.

Notice, 'faith' is the **'substance'** of the things we hope for. It is the tangible **'evidence'** of things we cannot see. We cannot see God, or His Power, but we certainly have the evidence that those Powers produced and sustain all tangible matter.

Material things that we can see and feel **are the evidence** of God's Powers which we cannot see.

*Hebrews 11:3 Through **faith** we understand that the worlds were framed by the word of God, so that things which are seen were not made of things which do appear.*

The gift of 'Faith' gives us the ability to 'see' and 'appreciate' that God is the Creator. No, the things we see all around us were not made of substance we can see, they were made of 'Spirit Substance' which we cannot see.

The rest of the chapter gives example after example of the faith of our forebears, and is always a source of encouragement to those who read it.

Belief: Christ gives us a definition of one type of God's Work in us, 'Belief'.

*John 6:28 Then said they unto him, What shall we do, that we might work the works of God? 29 Jesus answered and said unto them, **This is the work of God, that ye believe on him whom he hath sent.***

That could not be plainer. However, that measure of 'belief' is a gift of God. We can certainly 'believe' as humans, but the sort of 'belief' that Christ spoke of here is a Spiritual Gift.

Colossians 1:21 And you, that were sometime alienated and enemies in your mind by wicked works, yet now hath he reconciled 22 In the body of his flesh through death, to present you holy and unblameable and unreproveable in his sight:

23 If ye continue in the faith grounded and settled, and be not moved away from the hope of the gospel, which ye have heard, and which was preached to every creature which is under heaven; whereof I Paul am made a minister;

Christians can, and should show gratitude to God for the Sacrifice of Christ, who presents us pure white and blameless to His Father.

Galatians 2:20 I am crucified with Christ: nevertheless I live; yet not I, but Christ liveth in me: and the life which I now live in the flesh I live by the faith of the Son of God, who loved me, and gave himself for me.

Christ lives **in** us, and we **in** Him – Present continuous

Acts 17:38 For in him we live, and move, and have our being; as certain also of your own poets have said, For we are also his offspring.

Where are those of us who are true Christians now?

Ephesians 2:6 And hath raised us up together, and made us sit together in heavenly places in Christ Jesus: 7 That in the ages to come he might shew the exceeding riches of his grace in his kindness toward us through Christ Jesus.

Sitting at the Right Hand of the Father!

We eat food every day, and we need to study daily the Spiritual 'Bread of Life' too. Study of His Word not only nourishes our spirit, but also our bodies.

Matthew 4:4 But he (Christ) answered and said, It is written, Man shall not live by bread alone, but by every word that proceedeth out of the mouth of God.

We walk every day, and even walk for our health. Those who are in Christ are urged to walk with Him in the Spirit of Christian life. 'Walking' with Christ means to be aware moment by moment that we are with Him.

Galatians 5:16 This I say then, Walk in the Spirit, and ye shall not fulfil the lust of the flesh.

Galatians 5:25 If we live in the Spirit, let us also walk in the Spirit.

The more we walk in the Spirit, the easier it becomes to avoid fulfilling the lusts of the flesh.

*Colossians 1:10 That ye might **walk** worthy of the Lord unto all pleasing, being fruitful in every good work, and increasing in the knowledge of God;*

Christian Works are nothing to do with the Old Law. Salvation is a gift!

Many religious people are stuck with one foot in the Old Testament, and half a toe in the New Testament. In their religious lives, they attempt to keep the Mosaic Law of the first five books in the Bible, (which is actually totally impossible), not realising that in the process they are actually denying the sacrifice of Christ. It is sad that they cannot see that.

They fail to recognise that Christ came to 'fulfill' the Law, and bring in a New Era which supersedes the Old Mosaic Law with the New Spiritual Laws of Love which are a zillion times more difficult (actually completely impossible) to keep, than were the old physical laws.

The New Law of Love that Christ brought

When we look carefully at the 'Sermon on the Mount' with the help of the Holy Spirit, we can see clearly that this is Christ's exposition of showing that the old law has been superseded by His New Laws.

It is important to notice Christ's use of the word **BUT** which completely dismisses the words that precede it, clearly shows that the Old Laws are being replaced by a much more rigorous and spiritual form of the Law.

Notice that in every case, when the Old Law is quoted, it refers to the physical aspects and penalties for breaking it. Then Christ says, **BUT** this is not longer a physical issue, and goes on to explain the mental and spiritual responsibilities of the New Law.

He explains that it in 'old time' it was wrong to break the laws physically, **BUT** now, we are not even allowed to think in any way about anything that breaks the spirit of them!

*Matthew 5:21 Ye have heard that it was said of them of old time, Thou shalt not kill; and whosoever shall kill shall be in danger of the judgment: 22 **But** I say unto you, That whosoever is angry with his brother without a cause shall be in danger of the judgment: and whosoever shall say to his brother, Raca, shall be in danger of the council: but whosoever shall say, Thou fool, shall be in danger of hell (Strong's 1067 gehenna) (This is not the 'hell' taught by Christian ministers, but the constantlly burning tip of Jerusalem rubbish) fire (Strong's 4442 fire literally of figuratively)*

Christ here is upgrading the law, and saying, in the old days it was wrong to murder, **but** I am saying to you that you may not even be angry with anyone without just cause, (and even then you have to be most careful!).

*And in Matthew 5:27 Ye have heard that it was said by them of old time, Thou shalt not commit adultery: 28 **But** I say unto you, That whosoever looketh on a woman to lust after her hath committed adultery with her already in his heart.*

And in *Matthew 5:38 Ye have heard that it hath been said, An eye for an eye, and a tooth for a tooth: 39* **But** *I say unto you, That ye resist not evil: but whosoever shall smite thee on thy right cheek, turn to him the other also.*

And in *Matthew 5:43 Ye have heard that it hath been said, Thou shalt love thy neighbour, and hate thine enemy. 44* **But** *I say unto you, Love your enemies, bless them that curse you, do good to them that hate you, and pray for them which despitefully use you, and persecute you;*

Paul warned all of us who understand the teaching of "the Mystery":

Ephesians 5:5 For this you know, that no whoremonger, nor covetous man, who is an idolater, has any inheritance in the kingdom of Christ and of God.

If we do not please God the Father and Christ Jesus in our earthy lives, they may well consider it appropriate not to grant us our salvation until the thousand year "Kingdom phase" is over.

When people read in the New Testament of those who may not make it into their inheritance, it is always speaking about the "Kingdom phase" of salvation, not salvation itself which has been absolutely secured as a free gift to the human race through the works and efforts of Jesus Christ, our Elder Brother.

We should want to do good works now in order to please the Father and Christ. If we do, we can have the assurance that we will be in the first resurrection and enjoy along with Abraham, Moses, David, the apostles and others, the "Kingdom phase" of salvation. Let us remember, though all mankind is guaranteed a salvation through the works of Christ, all do not receive it at the same time

1 Timothy 2:4 Who will have all men to be saved, and to come unto the knowledge of the truth. 5 For there is one God, and one mediator between God and men, the man Christ Jesus; 6 Who gave himself a ransom for all, to be testified in due time.

But Paul said mankind will only be granted a salvation "in its own seasons" The original Greek in verse six makes it clear that salvation is awarded at different times.

We should always be diligent in doing good works. And we should also meet all our human obligations to our families, and to our societies that are within the boundaries of moral and ethical principles of fairness that are found within the biblical revelation.

Our legal and spiritual position of presently being on the right hand of the Father is a position only recognized by the Father and Christ Jesus. Mankind does not look on us Christians as having this august standing as the very children of God. So, all legitimate obligations we have with the rest of mankind should be fulfilled by Christians.

For example, if we have a contract to pay department store money for a product we received from them, we should pay the store precisely and meet all the obligations of the contract. True, any default will not jeopardize our salvation in Christ, but our wrong attitudes could keep us from experiencing the "Kingdom phase" of salvation and we can inherit many ills during this life by our wrongdoing. As will any of the 'works' of the flesh.

Galatians 5:16 This I say then, Walk (and Work) in the Spirit, and ye shall not fulfil the lust of the flesh. 17 For the flesh lusteth against the Spirit, and the Spirit against the flesh: and these are contrary the one to the other: so that ye cannot do the things that ye would. 18 But if ye be led of the Spirit, ye are not under the law. 19 Now the works of the flesh are manifest, which are these; Adultery, fornication, uncleanness, lasciviousness, 20 Idolatry, witchcraft, hatred, variance, emulations, wrath, strife, seditions, heresies, 21 Envyings, murders, drunkenness, revellings, and such like: of the which I tell you before, as I have also told you in time past, that they which do such things shall not inherit the kingdom of God.

What we should continually do, is to be trying to please the Father in our human actions by developing, and working with the gifts of the Spirit.

Galatians 5:22 But the fruit of the Spirit is love, joy, peace, longsuffering, gentleness, goodness, faith, 23 Meekness, temperance: against such there is no law. 24 And they that are Christ's have crucified the flesh with the affections and lusts. 25 If we live in the Spirit, let us also walk in the Spirit.

 But in spite of what our obligations are to others of the human race in this life, our spiritual obligations to the Father have been fully met in the actions of Christ Jesus on our behalf. When Christ was on earth He kept the Sabbath perfectly, as well as the Holyday celebrations, and all other ceremonial matters that God gave to Israel. He observed them as a substitute for us.

We have already kept all these ceremonial laws perfectly "in Christ" and they pertain to us no longer. Paul taught:

Colossians 2:16 Let no man therefore judge you in meat [food] or in drink, or in respect of an holyday, or of the new moon, or of the sabbath days: 17 which are a shadow of things to come [of future events].

We who understand "The Mystery" know that we have already kept all those ceremonial duties perfectly in Christ

CHRISTIAN WORKS AND THEIR REWARD

over 1900 years ago and we have satisfied God's require-ments in performing them fully. In fact, the whole of Christ's perfect life and all His works have now been attributed to us personally.

When we come before the judgment seat of God, the Father will simply look on our debit side and find no sins whatever accounted to us (they were paid for in full by Christ on our behalf) and when God looks at our credit side, He will find all the righteous works of Christ given (by grace) to us. His Works are now reckoned as our own works and we have already been judged perfect in respect of Salvation.

And as wonderful that is, we still want to focus on the prac-tical things we can do to store up our 'treasures in heaven', and hopefully qualify for entrance into the Kingdom of God, and reign with Christ for a thousand years, and more.

What about charitable work?
We live in a wicked world, run largely by unscrupulous, avaricious, unprincipled people. This is also true of the many 'registered' charities which consume most of the donations they receive in 'expenses' and very little actually reaches those the donor intended to give to.

Matthew 10:16 Behold, I send you forth as sheep in the midst of wolves: be ye therefore wise as serpents, and harmless as doves.

The adverts on television are excellent at portraying heart-rending scenes of children or animals living in terrible condi-tions, and others who suffer from this plight or another. Just a few dollars a month, they say, will help so many people. That might be true, and it might not be true. It might just be a scam to part you from your money.

To be on the safe side, keep a tight hold on your money or your assets, and only give to those you actually meet and have dealings with you. Even then, the principle is to 'prime the pump' only, and make it possible for the person to help themselves, for that is what God wants us all to do.

There is a well worn proverb that is not in the Bible, but it contains great truth: 'God helps those, who help themselves'.

Any money given to those who beg will probably quickly be spent on alcohol or drugs. Take the person to a food shop and buy them some fruit or a sandwich if you are moved by compassion. That way your 'work' will possibly be more helpful and effective.

Now when it comes to people you know well, and they are struggling Christians, then that is a different matter.

James 2:15 If a brother or sister be naked, and destitute of daily food, 16 And one of you say unto them, Depart in peace, be ye warmed and filled; notwithstanding ye give them not those things which are needful to the body; what doth it profit? 17 Even so faith, if it hath not works, is dead, being alone.

We need to be aware of the needs of people we know are members of the 'ecclesia', and if it is in our power, which it usually is to some extent or another, to help them in practical ways.

Do not be a surety for anyone.
Heed this advice from Solomon, the wisest man who live up until his time.

Never go 'surety' for anyone no matter if they are family, friend, or stranger. As soon as you sign on the dotted line, you are hooked. Not much fun if you are a fish either!

Proverbs 6:1 My son, if thou be surety for thy friend, if thou hast stricken thy hand with a stranger, 2 Thou art snared with the words of thy mouth, thou art taken with the words of thy mouth. 3 Do this now, my son, and deliver thyself, when thou art come into the hand of thy friend; go, humble thyself, and make sure thy friend. 4 Give not sleep to thine eyes, nor slumber to thine eyelids. 5 Deliver thyself as a roe from the hand of the hunter, and as a bird from the hand of the fowler.

Some charity work could well be an outlet for your time and effort. And, do not let yourself be taken advantage of to your detriment. Only do what you reasonably can within your time and your means.

Love one another; this is not always an easy 'work'.
One 'work' that is not always easy to perform is to love one another. Christ wants us to accept that it is our responsibility to love the unlovable, and to forgive those who despitefully use you. Not an easy task sometimes.

With help from Holy Spirit, we can be alert every day for ways we can be of service to others, and fulfil our continuous duty to be about our Father's business, and our own Christian works.

To sum up, the principle daily 'works' of a Christian are two fold:

To believe, **actively** *believe*, every day in the Lord Christ Jesus and His Work and His Sacrifice.

To walk in, and keep His Commandments of the New Law, as Christ defined them in the Sermon on the Mount and all the other clear definitions of His Commandments recorded by the Apostles throughout the New Testament.

The next chapter gives an exciting glimpse of our Glorious future in the Family of God.

CHRISTIAN WORKS AND THEIR REWARD

CHAPTER 7

THE MYSTERY REVEALED -
THE GREATEST TRUTH

Our Glorious Eternal Future as God's Children.

But as it is written, Eye hath not seen, nor ear heard, neither have entered into the heart of man, the things which God hath prepared for them that love him. But God hath revealed them unto us by his Spirit: for the Spirit searcheth all things, yea, the deep things of God.

1 Corinthians 2:9,10

The above is a quote from the Old Testament.
Isaiah 64:4 For since the beginning of the world men have not heard, nor perceived by the ear, neither hath the eye seen, O God, beside thee, what he hath prepared for him that waiteth for him.

Our future as human beings destined to inherit eternal life and become part of the Royal Family of the Almighty Creator God is beyond our comprehension, but the more we consider His Plan, the more real it becomes to us.

The majority of Christian people believe that the New Testament teaches that all Christians today are under what God calls "The New Covenant." Nothing could be farther from the truth.

Looking at Christians today in the manner that God the Father and how our Elder Brother Jesus Christ view Christians, no Christian is under either the "Old Covenant" or the "New Covenant."

Now wait a moment, before anyone thinks that statement heretical, a deeper look at the incredibly exciting New Testament teaching called by the apostle Paul "The Mystery" might help.

'The Mystery' was the final doctrine revealed by Christ Jesus to Paul and other apostles about the year 63 AD. That final revelation represents the finest teaching, the most exciting and inspiring that God could ever give to mankind. Sadly, it is a teaching that is almost totally misunderstood by Christian churches today.

This chapter will explain what the basic teaching of "The Mystery" actually entails, and it will then reveal where the teaching of the New Covenant fits into the Plan of God.

How do God and Christ Jesus view true Christians today?
The most important thing, however, is to determine how God the Father and Christ Jesus view the status of mature Christians today in a legal sense. Once we understand our legal standing with God in simple terms, we will then discover that mature Christian teaching is easy to understand, and makes perfectly good sense in a logical way.

The Apostle Paul's letters to the Ephesians and Colossians are companion letters and they speak about the 'Mystery' with slightly different emphases. 'The Mystery' in plain English simply means "The Secret".

This teaching of the 'Mystery' is described by Christ Jesus through Paul using several different terms.

*Ephesians 1:9 Having made known unto us the **mystery of his will**, according to his good pleasure which he hath purposed in himself:*

Here referred to as the 'mystery of his will', that is, God's Will for us.

*Ephesians 3:3 How that by revelation he made known unto me the mystery; (as I wrote afore in few words, 4 Whereby, when ye read, ye may understand my knowledge in the **mystery of Christ**)*

In verse 4 it is referred to as 'the Mystery of Christ'.

*Ephesians 3:9 And to make all men see what is **'the fellowship of the mystery'**, which from the beginning of the world hath been hid in God, who created all things by Jesus Christ:*

In verse 9 tells how all men and women, the ecclesia, is given "the fellowship of the mystery" in the King James Version, where 'fellowship' should be translated as 'administration', and so it is "The Administration of the Mystery". We are part of God's Administration team!

*Ephesians 5:32 This is a **great mystery**: but I speak concerning Christ and the church.*

In Ephesians 5:32 the Greek gives, 'The Great Mystery', that as 'husband and wife are one', so all true Christians are 'One *in* Christ'. Christ's body of believers, the Greek *ekklesia* is erroneously translated in the Bible and here as "church".

*Colossians 2:2 That their hearts might be comforted, being knit together in love, and unto all riches of the full assurance of understanding, to the acknowledgement of **the mystery of God, and of the Father, and of Christ**;*

Here, Christ through Paul says the 'The Mystery of God, the Father, and Christ".

This "Great Mystery" or "Secret" was made known to Paul and the 'ecclesia' about the year 63 A.D., and from that time onward this doctrine was made known through the ecclesia to the whole world and also to all the angelic powers throughout the earth and the heavens

Ephesians 3:9 And to make all men see what is the fellowship of the mystery, which from the beginning of the world hath been hid in God, who created all things by Jesus Christ: 10 To the intent that now unto the principalities and powers in heavenly places might be known by the church ecclesia the manifold wisdom of God, 11 According to the eternal purpose which he purposed in Christ Jesus our Lord:

Before 63 A.D., the apostle Paul said the Mystery "had been hid in God". God had kept it a secret from the knowledge of anyone, human beings, or angelic principalities and powers in heaven and earth.

The secret kept even from before the foundation of the world, long before the creation of Adam. Indeed, Paul said that "from the beginning of the world [Gk. eons, or ages, plural] it has been hid in God" (verse 9). Paul spoke of it as "... the Mystery of Christ which in other ages was not made known unto the sons of men, as it is NOW [in 63 AD] revealed unto his holy apostles and prophets by the Spirit."

Ephesians 3:5 Which in other ages was not made known unto the sons of men, as it is now revealed unto his holy apostles and prophets by the Spirit;

Repeated for emphasis in Colossians:

Colossians 1:26 Even the mystery which hath been hid from ages and from generations, but now is made manifest to his saints:

The incredible picture of our future which this new information brings is breathtaking! Christ in us, and we in Christ, all One, ruling the Universe and everything Christ created, with the Father, for ever.

This certainly beats the unbiblical notion most Christians cling to of going to heaven when they die, or sitting on a cloud strumming a harp!

Colossians 1:27 To whom God would make known what is the riches of the glory of this mystery among the Gentiles; which is Christ in you, the hope of glory:

We ordinary human beings are to inherit eternal life as fully fledged Children of God, being an integral part of the God Family. Is this incredible or what? And it is true!!!

This brand new revelation called "The Mystery, which from the beginning of the world [Gk. eons, plural] has been hid in God" (Ephesians 3:9) There is nothing about the "Mystery teaching" in any of the earlier epistles of Paul except in the postscript at the very end of Romans after he says 'Amen', which was written after 63 A.D.

Romans 16:25 Now to him that is of power to stablish you according to my gospel, and the preaching of Jesus Christ, according to the revelation of the mystery, which was kept secret since the world began, 26 But now is made manifest, and by the scriptures of the prophets, according to the commandment of the everlasting God, made known to all nations for the obedience of faith: 27 To God only wise, be glory through Jesus Christ for ever. Amen.

Which, notice, that this repeats once again the important statement that the 'Mystery' had been kept secret since the world (aeons - times) began. Repetition again for emphasis.

This new teaching was not known by the apostles, the early Christians or the Jews in any period earlier than 63 A.D. Adam did not know of it. Abraham was unaware of it.

Moses did not hear it. Christ did not teach it to the Jews or his disciples while he was on earth. The apostles themselves from 30 A.D., (when the first Jewish ecclesia began on Pentecost day after Christ's resurrection) and up to the year 63 AD (33 years later) did not know of this advanced and final teaching of the Gospel either.

It was only when special revelations were given byChrist to Paul and then to others in and after that crucial year of 63 A.D., that this grandest teaching that God could ever give to mankind was revealed. And it was something very different from what had been taught before, even in matters involving Christian belief and the Christian faith.

New information for Christians, yet 'lost' to the world.
From 63 AD onward, "The Mystery" put Christians into an entirely different legal status to God the Father and our Elder Brother Jesus Christ. Yet, the thousands of the churches of 'Churchianity' do not appear to appreciate the amazing truth of the 'Mystery' or teach it. Extraordinary blindness!

Its revelation elevated Christians to a sublime and high position in the Divine Hierarchy in heaven. The religious laws, rules, and statutes that were designed to govern various races of mankind (while they are reckoned as humans in the flesh) were entirely superseded by a new spiritual status. This legal position completely eliminated the need for any religious physical rules, rites, or practices to be observed by Christians.

In a word, a brand new legal status was given to those humans who now found themselves as being spiritually actually "**in** Christ Jesus." It is now time that the importance of this knowledge, and what this new legal status is all about, is published to the world at large to those whose minds are opened to understand it by God.

The incredible 'Rank' of the true Christian today.

By being "in Christ Jesus" (in the manner meant in the teaching of "the Mystery"), true Christians are appointed to have a Divine position of immense rank and importance in the eyes of the Father, even though we are still human beings and are still living in the flesh on this earth. It is the most wonderful and glorious instruction ever given to mankind or to the angelic hosts in earth or in heaven.

The "New Covenant" teaching of the first thirty years of Christianity is excellent and beautiful in its scope, and will still have relevance in the future. However, the teaching of "The Mystery" changes the initial legal status of Christians, now to be reckoned as a mere glimmer of light compared to the principles of "The Mystery" that emblazon forth with the full strength of the meridian sun. The revelation of the 'Mystery' was a giant leap forward in understanding.

It takes a Christian from being considered "a glorified human" into a prestigious legal position of being reckoned by the Father as "a glorified God", with the Christian having an equal family status, but not the degree of Power of course, alongside the Father and Christ Jesus.

Simply put, to be "in Christ Jesus" in the teaching of "The Mystery" carries with it a profound meaning and legal significance in the eyes of the Father. Here are the basic tenets of this new teaching called "The Mystery" that was kept secret from the knowledge of the world until the apostles revealed it about the year 63 A.D.

What was entailed in the teachings of "The Mystery"? The first principle of "The Mystery" is that Christians now are no longer reckoned by the Father as either a Jew or a Gentile. Under the New Covenant legislation there were still various rules of religious conduct that Jewish Christians and Gentile Christians were expected to observe. Indeed, all Gentile Christians had to become a part of the nation of Israel and were expected to perform the religious duties of Israelites (except physical circumcision and other such exclusive Jewish rituals of the flesh).

But with "The Mystery," Christians are no longer seen by the Father as either a Jew or a Gentile. All physical and religious distinctions that made Jews and Gentiles to be separate peoples have been abolished in, and superseded by "The Mystery".

Ephesians 2:11 Wherefore remember, that ye being in time past Gentiles in the flesh, who are called Uncircumcision by that which is called the Circumcision in the flesh made by hands; 12 That at that time ye were without Christ, being aliens from the commonwealth of Israel, and strangers from the covenants of promise, having no hope, and without God in the world: 13 But **now** *in Christ Jesus ye who sometimes were far off are made nigh by the blood of Christ. 14 For he is our peace, who hath made both (Jew and Gentile) one, and hath broken down the middle wall of partition between us;*

Christians are a 'New Race' of Human Beings
A new status is now in effect for true Christians.

Ephesians 2:15 Having abolished in his flesh the enmity, even the law of commandments contained in ordinances; **for** *to make in himself of twain (two races) one new man, so making peace; 16 And that he might reconcile both (human races) unto God in one body by the cross, having slain the enmity thereby: 17 And came and preached peace to you which were afar off, and to them that were nigh.*

This "NEW MAN" is neither Jew nor Gentile. In fact, "A NEW RACE OF PERSONS" has been created. Now, both Jewish Christians and Gentile Christians have been melded together into ONE BODY, the body of Christ. A new legal status with the Father has emerged.

What are Christians - since 63 AD – NOW today?

Perhaps those who read this will need to 'hang on to their hats'!

Ephesians 2:18 For through him (Christ) we both have access by one Spirit unto the Father. 19 Now therefore ye are no more strangers and foreigners, but fellowcitizens with the saints, and of the household of God;

We are part of the 'household of God' Where is the 'household of God'? It is where God lives, in heaven! Legally we are already there in Spirit.

Ephesians 2:20 And are built upon the foundation of the apostles and prophets, Jesus Christ himself being the chief corner stone;21 In whom all the building fitly framed together groweth unto an holy temple in the Lord:

Christ's body and the ecclesia together, (that is us!) form a place, a special Temple for God to live in!

Colossians 2:22 In whom ye also are builded together for an habitation of God through the Spirit.

We are part of the household and habitation of God in a very real sense, right now! Sitting at the right hand of the Father with Christ Jesus in whom are live and have our being.

Colossians 3:1 If ye then be risen with Christ, seek those things which are above, where Christ sitteth on the right hand of God.

Astonishing that in a very real but symbolic, spiritual sense, we are in heaven now!

Acts 17:28 For in him (Christ) we live, and move, and have our being; as certain also of your own poets have said, For we are also his offspring.

We are already His offspring, that is actual children of Christ and God.

What Is the Prime Teaching of the Mystery? The central teaching of "The Mystery" is that Christians have Christ **in** them, and that all Christians are also **in** Christ. Christ is now **in** us and we are **in** Him.

Here is how Paul worded it in Colossians:

Colossians 1:27 God would make known what is the riches of the glory of this mystery among the Gentiles [even the Gentiles would know of it]; which is CHRIST IN YOU, the hope of glory [the hope of achieving a divine glory]: 28 whom we preach, warning every man and teaching every man in all wisdom; that we may present EVERY MAN PER-FECT IN CHRIST JESUS.

So, the teaching of "the Mystery" is that EVERY MAN [every human being male and female] will finally understand that he or she is **in** (part of) Christ Jesus; and that EVERY MAN [every human, male or female] is also to have Christ Jesus in himself or herself [Christ Jesus is eventually to be found in all mankind]!

How long have we Christians been in this Legal Position?
How long have Christians been in this Legal position? This is a most important aspect of the teaching of "the Mystery."

When did we first obtain all our spiritual blessings "in Christ"? Paul said:

Ephesians 1:4 According as he [God] has chosen us in him [Christ] before the foundation of the world (Greek kosmos).

Our being "in Christ" was made legal in the eyes of the Father even before the physical cosmos which we see around us came into existence. This was the Glory of God's Plan. We were then given the legal status of being reckoned as the very children of God Himself.

Ephesians 1:5 Having predestinated us unto the adoption of children by Jesus Christ to himself, according to the good pleasure of His will.

The word translated here *'predestinated' is Strong's 4309 pro-or-id'-zo; from (4253) (pro>) and (3724) (oJri>zw); to limit in advance, i.e. (figurative) predetermine: — determine before, ordain, predestinate.*

God and His Son, the Word who became Christ, planned our adoption into His family before the Creation of the entire physical Universe.

What is 'predestined', and how did that come about?

So we who are the adopted children of God, each of us was 'determined before', 'ordained' to be given that position. But how did that happen?

God has His way of doing things, in most cases that is not the human way. But in this instance, how 'predestination' actually occurred and when may surprise you especially if you are not aware of the principle.

In the book of Acts, it records how a replacement Apostle was chosen to replace Judas who died very shortly after betraying Christ. How Judas died is explained in Acts 1. There were originally twelve apostles, then after Judas died, only eleven, so someone had to be found to replace Judas, and this is how it happened.

Acts 1:20 For it is written in the book of Psalms, Let his habitation be desolate, and let no man dwell therein: and his bishoprick let another take.

Firstly, Acts records that the replacement for Judas was prophesied in the Psalms.

Acts 1:21 Wherefore of these men which have companied with us all the time that the Lord Jesus went in and out among us, 22 Beginning from the baptism of John, unto that same day that he was taken up from us, must one be ordained to be a witness with us of his resurrection.

The first qualification to become an Apostle at that time was that the person had to have been with the twelve all the time Christ was with them, and a witness of His resurrection.

Acts 1:23 And they appointed two, Joseph called Barsabas, who was surnamed Justus, and Matthias. 24 And they prayed, and said, Thou, Lord, which knowest the hearts of all men, shew whether of these two thou hast chosen, 25 That he may take part of this ministry and apostleship, from which Judas by transgression fell, that he might go to his own place.

Having prayed about it, look now at the surprising way that the choice was made.

*Acts 1:26 And they gave forth their **lots**; and **the lot** fell upon Matthias; and he was numbered with the eleven apostles.*

'Lot', *Strong's 2819 Greek klay'-ros; probably from (2806) (kla>w) (through the idea of using bits of wood, etc., for the purpose); a die (for drawing chances); by implication a portion (as if so secured); by extension an acquisition (especially a patrimony, figurative):* — *heritage, inheritance, lot, participle*

Notice the extended meanings of the Greek word *klay-ros* include using pieces of wood to draw by chance, for a heritage, or inheritance.

They cast lots to decide which of the two men should replace Judas. This principle was well known to the Apostles. Notice Peter said the elders should not lord it over their congregations who were those selected by 'lot'.

*1 Peter 5:3 Neither as being lords over God's ~~heritage~~ **lot** (Greek, klay-ros - lot) but being examples to the flock.*

Peter was inspired to use the same word *klay-ros* incorrectly translated here as 'heritage', as was used in Acts 1 telling of casting lots, the same word.

The Bible does not say exactly how this was done, but a lottery it was! And in a sense it was random. In modern day lotteries, there are many balls in a container being blown about, until one, then another falls completely at random.

This is important as we look carefully at the word 'predestinated', and when this 'heritage' or 'inheritance' occurred for us.

Ephesians 1:11 In whom also we have obtained an ~~inheritance~~ lot (Greek klay-roo) Being predestinated according to the purpose of him who worketh all things after the counsel of his own will:

Strong's 2820 klhro>w, — klay-ro'-o; from (2819) (klh~rov); to allot, i.e (figurative) to assign (a privilege): — obtain an inheritance.

Notice that the 'lot' was cast according to the Will of God.

CHRISTIANITY DIRECT FROM CHRIST – THE WORD OF GOD

*Colossians 1:12 Giving thanks unto the Father, which hath made us meet to be partakers of the **inheritance** (lot - Greek klay-ros) of the saints in light:*

The word 'inheritance' here is the same word in Acts translated 'lot' cast to choose Matthias.

When were people allotted by God's Lottery to be chosen?
Ephesians 1:4 According as he hath **chosen** us in him **before** the foundation of the world, that we should be holy and without blame before him in love:

How were we 'chosen' and when? By 'lot', and before the foundation of the world or kosmos!

*Acts 17:4 And some of them believed, and ~~consorted~~ **allotted** with Paul and Silas; and of the devout Greeks a great multitude, and of the chief women not a few.*

*The word 'consorted' is once again a Greek word meaning 'lot' or 'allotted'. Strong's 4345) pros-klay-ro'-o; from (4314) (pro>v) and (2820) (klhro>w); **to give a common lot to**, i.e. (figurative) to associate with: — consort with.*

So the 'called' to be Christians then and now were 'allotted' to this position aeons ago! Everything is according to the counsel of God's Will. We need the gift of faith to **believe** and **know** that everything is working out as God planned it to happen.

*2 Peter 1:1 Simon Peter, a servant and an apostle of Jesus Christ, to them that have ~~obtained~~ **received by lot** like precious faith with us through the righteousness of God and our Saviour Jesus Christ:*

Strong's 2975 greek lagca>nw, — lang-khan'-o; a prolonged form of a primary verb, to lot, i.e. determine (by implication receive) especially by lot: — his lot be, cast lots, obtain.

232   **THE MYSTERY REVEALED -   THE GREATEST TRUTH**

In all these cases, the King James translators had no idea whatsoever that the reason Paul then, or we now, could understand these 'secrets' of the Mystery was because we had been chosen at the pre-creation time by God's Lottery!

Why was God's lottery random? It was for a very important reason indeed.

We need to be very clear about an important Characteristic of our Wonderful God of Love. But before we go into the reason for 'God's Lottery', there is something that is largely hidden from 'Churchianity'. If those who have sought to understand Christianity only understood this aspect of God, life would be a lot easier for many people who cannot comprehend why God allows all the evil in the world.

God is the Almighty God, and as such He is in charge of all that happens in the Universe. There is absolutely nothing that occurs within the Heavenly or the Earthly realms that God is not supervising. God is in complete control of EVERYTHING. This Power is summed up in Chronicles.

1 Chronicles 19:11 Thine, O LORD is the greatness, and the power, and the glory, and the victory, and the majesty: for all that is in the heaven and in the earth is thine; thine is the kingdom, O LORD, and thou art exalted as head above all. 12 Both riches and honour come of thee, and thou reignest over all; and in thine hand is power and might; and in thine hand it is to make great, and to give strength unto all.

We really have to understand and appreciate that our God the Creator creates all things.

Isaiah 45:5 I am the LORD, and there is none else, there is no God beside me: I girded thee, though thou hast not known me: 6 That they may know from the rising of the sun, and from the west, that there is none beside me. I am the LORD, and there is none else. 7 I form the light, and *create darkness: **I make peace, and create evil:** I the LORD do all these things.*

God creates peace and He Creates Evil

To be clear, the LORD speaking here on behalf of the Father is the Word who became Christ. Christ created Satan under the instructions of the Father. This might sound ridiculous to some, but the Bible plainly teaches that is true. There is no contest, God the Father and Christ are in control of **everything** that happens. That is a hard concept for most churchgoers to accept.

So powerful is God that Satan the Devil obeys every command that God gives him.

Job 1:6 Now there was a day when the sons of God came to present themselves before the LORD, and Satan came also among them. 7 And the LORD said unto Satan, Whence comest thou? Then Satan answered the LORD, and said, From going to and fro in the earth, and from walking up and down in it....12 And the LORD said unto Satan, Behold, all that he hath is in thy power; only upon himself put not forth thine hand. So Satan went forth from the presence of the LORD.

God gave Satan instructions, and Satan carried them out to the letter. Again in Job 2:1-8, Satan followed God's orders exactly.

Yes, God created 'evil' along with everything else He created. Accepting and understanding this will help us understand our God and Christ Jesus so much better.

God can and does Create Evil, and He uses evil in any way He chooses in order to fulfil His Purpose and ensure the 'good' outcome He intends.

The greatest evil, the greatest and worst bad thing to happen on Earth was the crucifixion of Christ which was planned and happened with the foreknowledge of the Father and Christ Jesus aeons before it happened. The exact details of that occurrence were prophesied to happen exactly as they did with all the 'players' playing their parts in the whole event before the foundation of the world.

Without God's use of Evil for 'good', we would not have a Saviour from the penalty of our sins, we would not have an inheritance by lot to become fully fledged Children of God.

What an incredible privilege it is for us who have been chosen 'by lot' to be able to understand this now, today, and that we are able to have the opportunity to appreciate this concept of 'good' and 'evil' as we look more closely at 'God's Lottery'.

As we come to understand this principle, the reason that things are the way they are in this wonderful but excruciating world we live in will become clearer.

So in God's Lottery, some people are appointed to do evil, and others to do 'good'.

A deeper knowledge of how God conducted 'His Lottery' will help to provide answers to the many questions people have about 'why' some people tend to be 'evil' and others appear to be more 'good'.

One thing we do need to realise is that God is scrupulously Fair and Just. It will help is if we ask for God to grant us the gifts of belief, acceptance, and faith in His Absolute Fairness.

The Apostle Paul explains in the clearest of terms that Jacob was 'elected' or 'allotted' to be loved by God before he was born, and Esau was 'elected' or 'allotted' to be hated (loved less) by God.

Romans 9:10 And not only this; but when Rebecca also had conceived by one, even by our father Isaac; 11 (For the children being not yet born, neither having done any good or evil, that the purpose of God according to election (Gk. Divine selection) might stand, not of works, but of him that calleth;) 12 It was said unto her, The elder shall serve the younger. 13 As it is written, Jacob have I loved, but Esau have I hated.

This to our human minds certainly does appear to be 'unfair', but only if we look at this in our limited human way, rather than in God's unlimited way, where everything He does will work out for everyone's Glorious benefit in the end.

Romans 9:14 What shall we say then? Is there unrighteousness with God? God forbid. 15 For he saith to Moses, I will have mercy on whom I will have mercy, and I will have compassion on whom I will have compassion.

God in His infinite Wisdom, and in a display of His Power, has mercy on some and compassion on others.

Romans 9:16 So then it is not of him that willeth, nor of him that runneth, but of God that sheweth mercy. 17 For the scripture saith unto Pharaoh, Even for this same purpose have I raised thee up, that I might shew my power in thee, and that my name might be declared throughout all the earth.

God raised up Pharoah for the express purpose of preventing the Israelites from leaving Egypt by hardening his heart.

Romans 9:18 Therefore hath he mercy on whom he will have mercy, and whom he will he hardeneth.

God chose Pharaoh by lot before the world was for this express purpose.

Romans 9:19 Thou wilt say then unto me, Why doth he yet find fault? For who hath resisted his will? 20 Nay but, O man, who art thou that repliest against God? Shall the thing formed say to him that formed it, Why hast thou made me thus?

Should any of us say of ourselves or indeed should anyone else ask, "Why hast thou made me thus?"

*Romans 9:21 Hath not the potter power over the clay, of the same lump to make one vessel unto **honour**, and another unto **dishonour**?*

So what about the worst, most evil people we know of? What of Genghis Kahn, Hitler, Pol Pot, and all the other consummately evil, despotic, cruel leaders of countries of our present evil world? They were predestined, allotted for their roles as 'evil' people, to have that tendency, according to God's Will.

Romans 9:22 What if God, willing to shew his wrath, and to make his power known, endured with much longsuffering the vessels of wrath fitted to destruction:

And what about all the 'good' people in the world doing their best to be kind, do good works, and treat others with kindness and love? That is the role to which they were 'allotted'. That is the way they are constructed to have that tendency to God's Glory. This is why we should never 'boast' of our efforts to be good.

One of the main reasons we are on this Earth as humans at this time, is to attend this 'school' for our entire lives, and the main lesson to be learned by everyone is about the difference between 'good' and 'evil'.

The Serpent in the Garden of Eden was doing God's Will when he persuaded Eve to eat of the tree of the knowledge of 'good' and 'evil'. It was God's initial step to educate His first children to know the difference between 'good' and 'evil' right from the beginning! This was His Plan, so that after His Son brought Salvation to all, God could raise every human being to Glory.

Romans 9:23 And that he might make known the riches of his glory on the vessels of mercy, which he had afore prepared unto glory,

Paul went on to state that God the Father had deliberately blinded the eyes of most Israelites in Christ's day to prevent them from accepting Him.

Romans 11:25 For I would not, brethren, that ye should be ignorant of this mystery, lest ye should be wise in your own conceits; that blindness in part is happened to Israel, until the fulness of the Gentiles be come in.

We are still in this time frame! The world is still blinded to the truth until the full appointed number of the Gentiles comes into their preordained relationship with God. He has not abandoned Israel at all, as the promised salvation for them will come.

Romans 11:26 And so all Israel shall be saved: as it is written, There shall come out of Sion the Deliverer, and shall turn away ungodliness from Jacob:

All Israelites, every single one of them, Jews, and all the other Tribes will one day be saved in Christ. They have been promised Salvation, and they will receive it, absolutely. This is the plain teaching of the Bible.

Romans 11:27 For this is my covenant unto them, when I shall take away their sins. 28 As concerning the gospel, they are enemies for your sakes: but as touching the election, they are beloved for the father's sakes. 29 For the gifts and calling of God are without repentance (on God's part). 30 For as ye in times past have not believed God, yet have now obtained mercy through their unbelief: 31 Even so have these also now not believed, that through your mercy they also may obtain mercy. 32 For God hath concluded them all in unbelief, that he might have mercy upon all.

God knows they are all in 'unbelief' so that He can have mercy on them in time to come. This realisation caused Paul to exclaim:

Romans 11:33 O the depth of the riches both of the wisdom and knowledge of God! how unsearchable are his judgments, and his ways past finding out 34 For who hath known the mind of the Lord? or who hath been his counsellor.

Wow! What an honour and a privilege it is for us to be given the opportunity now, right now, to understand more clearly the Plan of God which is hidden from 'Churchianity' because of their blindness, and their resistance to God's way of life for Christians.

People and Nations are still 'elected', 'allotted' to be blinded or not.

Some people and indeed whole nations were 'elected' when the 'Divine Lottery' was cast before the foundation of the world to have a chance to accept the truth now.

Others were elected by the same 'Divine Lottery' to be negative in their attitude towards the truth of the Gospel for now.

The Lottery was the completely fair way assigning all people an equal chance of being selected to do the Will of God. Whether to do 'good' or 'evil' in regard to specific events they were preordained in God's Plan to deal with in their lives, for the redemption of the human race to Himself.

When one surveys the Holy Scriptures regarding this principle of using the 'Divine Lottery' to determine who was to do what and at what time in history, then we can see the absolute fairness and equality of God in action among all the people He was going to Create, and cause to become His Children.

The outcome of such a 'lottery' could have fallen on Japheth, or upon Ham, instead of falling to the favour of Shem and his descendants. Shem and his children, by pure chance, were 'allotted' to have the fulness of the teaching of God, and through them to bring forth the Messiah who would arise to save the world from their sins.

This is why none of us should 'boast' about our 'calling' now! We are just the lucky ones who won that role in the lottery! And it is not because of any 'righteousness' of our own.

When we look at the lives of Jacob, or David in the Scriptures, they did some very bad things, that could cause any normal person to wonder why God would pick them; when there were other individuals in their time who were far better people in character. Yet God picked them because the 'Lot' had fallen on them to do the work He had appointed to them, regardless of their faults.

And so it is with all of us in this 21st Century, we are being given this opportunity now, because the 'lot' fell on us, regardless of all our faults and failings, which God does not see, as Christ presents each of us to the Father faultless.

We were not there at the time back then, but God and Christ knew what each of us would become personally in precise detail. And at just the right moment, designed by God, He sent out a call to each or us personally to respond to the Gospel message, and 'to come to a knowledge of the truth'. We had nothing to do with it! That is why everything about our election and calling comes to us by Grace.

Meanwhile for the moment, others are:

2 Timothy 3:7 Ever learning, and never able to come to the knowledge of the truth.

And it is not their 'fault' in any way shape or form, their time has not yet come! It is important to respect that this is God's Will for them at this time.

People are not saved to be 'bad'. They are saved to do 'good'.

This present life on Earth is a learning experience for all who make up the human race. We are here to gain experience of 'good' and 'evil' (which simply means 'bad'). Being able to recognise the difference and the consequences during our lives, whether short or long is our aim.

This will create in each of us a realisation of what is 'good' and 'bad', and that it always pays to practice 'good' and to refrain from the 'bad' or 'evil'. It is the ability to recognise that it is this difference that makes us like God. In this way all humans are becoming more like God all the time whether they realise it or not!

One day in the resurrection, when humans become full members of the Divine Family, they will always be doing 'good' in pleasing God. God speed that day!

This divine position of being accounted as God's own children was accomplished by Christ "according to the good pleasure of His will", not by our own wills. Indeed, we did not even exist at the time.

But so certain was this divine status assured to us, that the apostle Paul even concluded that each of us was already saved "in Christ" long before Adam was ever created.

2 Timothy 1:9 Who has saved (past tense) us, and called us with an holy calling, not according to our works, but according to His own purpose and grace, which was given us in Christ before the world [eonian times] began.

We were considered to be in Christ even at that distant time in the past. But it does not end there.

When Christ came into this world and became a human baby, we were also reckoned by the Father to have been "in Christ" at that time too.

How can we know this? Because eight days after Christ's birth he was circumcised in the Temple at Jerusalem. And what does Paul say of this act as far as our legal relationship to Christ was concerned?

Colossians 2:11 In whom [in Christ] also you are circumcised with the circumcision made without hands, in putting off the body of the sins of the flesh by the circumcision of Christ"

In other words, when Christ was circumcised as a baby of eight days, you and I, whether male or female makes no difference for this is a religious and legal principle for human beings being discussed here. We were also 'circumcised' in the eyes of the Father at the same time! But it still does not end there.

We continued in a legal sense to be "in Christ" for about thirty years until the time of Jesus Christ's baptism by John the Baptist. And then what happened according to Paul? That is when each of us was unitedly "buried with him in baptism"

Colossians 2:12 Buried with him in baptism, wherein also ye are risen with him through the faith of the operation of God, who hath raised him from the dead.

The truth is, Paul was telling the Colossians (and all of us) that when John the Baptist was baptizing Christ for sins, it was not Christ's sins that were being washed away (because He had none personally). It was our sins that were legally being washed away. Since we were then "in Christ," we were vicariously accounted by the Father as being baptized when John baptized Christ.

Ephesians 4:5 One Lord, one faith, one baptism,

This means that legally each of us has been baptized in the River Jordan by no lesser person than John the Baptist himself! This is the "one baptism" that now counts in your salvation, not the one (or ones) performed on you by some other humans here on earth. But it doesn't end there.

When Christ died on the tree of crucifixion, you were still "in Christ" at that time too. Paul said even before the teaching of "the Mystery" that

Galatians 2:20 I am crucified with Christ: nevertheless I live; yet not I, but Christ lives in me.

This means that when Christ died by crucifixion, the Father reckons that you died with Him because you were "in Christ" at the time. But it doesn't end there.

When Christ rose from the dead three days later, you also rose up with Him! As Paul taught:

Colossians 3:1 If ye then be risen with Christ, seek those things which are above, where Christ sitteth on the right hand of God.

That is right! When Christ was risen from the dead, the Father legally reckoned that you also were risen from the dead at the same time.

There is more.

Not only that, since after death all people are destined to be resurrected and go to the judgment of God which Christ did.

Hebrews 9:27 And as it is appointed unto men once to die, but after this the judgment:

So likewise Christ went through a judgment after His death (as all humans must do), and He passed through triumphantly.

And what did the Father do with Christ after He passed His judgment with no sins on His records (only perfect obedience was recorded)?

The Father told Christ to come forward and sit on His right hand.

Ephesians 1:20 Which he wrought in Christ, when he raised him from the dead, and set him at his own right hand in the heavenly places, 21 Far above all principality, and power, and might, and dominion, and every name that is named, not only in this world, but also in that which is to come.

This was all fine for Christ, what about you and me? What is wonderful is the teaching of "the Mystery" that you and I were also "in Christ" even at that time. And if you are a Christian, right now today! We are in the same exalted position as Our Elder Brother because we are **IN** Him.

In the eyes of the Father each of us went triumphantly with Christ through the judgment and sat down with Him on the right hand of the Father Himself. That is right, you and I are still "in Christ" and we are presently sitting (and I mean in a legal and spiritual sense right at this very moment) on that very throne in heaven.

Paul said:

Ephesians 2:5 [God] has quickened us together [made us alive together] with Christ, (by grace are you saved), and has raised us up together, and made us sit together in heavenly places in Christ Jesus.

Billions think they will to go to heaven when they die, but if they are true Christians, they are already there in Spirit!

We are considered to be in heaven where Christ sits at the right hand of God.

Colossians 3:1 If ye then be risen with Christ, seek those things which are above, where Christ sitteth on the right hand of God.

We have passed our judgment with Him and are legally sitting in Him, and He in us at the right hand of the Father! When the Father looks over to His right and sees Christ sitting there beside Him as His own firstborn of all creation, the Father also sees each of us (in a very personal way) legally sitting there with Him.

That we were and are:

'born' with Him;

'circumcised' with Him,

'baptised' with him;

'died' with him;

'resurrected' with Him;

'judged' with Him;

'accepted as pure and Holy in God's sight' with Him;

*'now live **in** Him*

That is what the teaching of "The Mystery" is all about! Wow!

Christ was the Firstborn of the Father, we are *in* Him so we are also Firstborn Children of God.

The Father has no second born children. He only has firstborn! Each of us are (and soon the whole human race once they are redeemed will be) sitting in that same firstborn position "in Christ" in the very family of the living God! That's why Paul said in the teaching of "the Mystery" that each of us makes up "the household of God."

We are a part of the divine family of God which controls and governs the entirety of this universe. Our destiny (even before the creation of Adam) has been to become the very adopted children of God! And each of us will perform that role because of the works of Christ on our behalf.

We have been saved "in Christ" from before the foundation of the physical cosmos.

2 Timothy 1:9 Who hath saved us, and called us with an holy calling, not according to our works, but according to his own purpose and grace, which was given us in Christ Jesus before the world began,

And though the Father kept the understanding of this divine truth a secret from the beginning of time, He saw fit to give that knowledge to the world in 63 AD through His apostles, and to those whose eyes are open right now.

Our Present Obligations, Our salvation in Christ is assured. It has been certain because we were "in Christ" before Adam was created. That is why the apostle Paul said that our salvation is something that is given to us by grace (long before our births) and not by any works of man (whether those works be good or bad).

True enough, works were essential in securing our salvation, but they were not our works, they were the works of Christ Jesus while He was in the flesh over 1900 years ago. He is the one who did the perfect works for us as our substitute.

Where so many Christians go wrong today is in their belief that they have to do some works (many are not sure just what works) in order to be saved.

Some think they have to work up a measure of "faith" on their own. Nonsense! Any faith you have to work up to believe in Christ is going to be a deficient work, because you simply cannot work up enough faith on your own to get you saved. Faith in this context is a gift of God, not a human ability at all.

Salvation is truly dependent upon works, but those works happen to be those of Jesus Christ who completed them for us while He was on earth. He lived a life of substitution for us, and God the Father accepts that substitutionary role of Christ in our stead as the means to give us a Perfect righteousness and sinlessness in His sight. Christ did the works that got us saved.

The teaching of "the Mystery" is not a teaching about what you have to do for you to get saved. It is a teaching that shows you and the world what Christ Jesus did that got you and the world saved. What preachers need to do today is give the world the Christian teaching of what Jesus Christ did for them to get them saved, not what they supposedly have to do to get saved.

*Ephesians 2:8 For by grace are ye **saved** (past tense) through faith; and that not of yourselves: it is the gift of God:*

True, all people must express a belief and faith in Christ. They must also will in their hearts to repent and live the proper ethical and moral way that Christ approves for His people. But even here, what people misunderstand is the fact that the apostle Paul said:

Philippians 2:13 it is God which works in you both to will and to do of his good pleasure.

Even when we **will** to do good works, it is something motivated by God from the action of His grace [as a gift] to us.

Our own 'good works' have no relevance in securing a salvation for us. Only the works of Christ which He did perfectly for us are the works that God the Father will accept in the matter of our salvation. That is why our salvation is secure, because it is not our works that count in granting us salvation. It is the works of Christ that He did for us in His substitutionary role of living, dying and being resurrected in our stead.

A warning! While our salvation is assured, we should always be about our Father's business and living in a righteous way that contributes to the glory of Christ Jesus. We should always be pleasing Christ and the Father with an upright and proper conduct of life. You will have read in Chapter 6 what works a Christian is urged to do in their daily lives, and what is the wonderful reward for those works.

On the other hand, if we decide to live like those in the world do after knowing this wonderful truth of "the Mystery," we can miss out on the Millennial Kingdom phase of salvation.

Ephesians 5:5 For this ye know, that no whoremonger, nor unclean person, nor covetous man, who is an idolater, hath any inheritance in the kingdom of Christ and of God.

So if anyone continues to live like the rest of the world, they will be brought to salvation all right, but God will let them inherit salvation with the rest of the world, when the world gets their salvation "in Christ." The people of the world obtains their salvation only after the Kingdom phase of a thousand years reign of Christ is over in the second resurrection.

But, if God and Christ are delighted with our conduct in this life, they will resurrect us in the first resurrection and embrace us to enjoy the Millennial Kingdom phase of salvation

Revelation 20:4 And I saw thrones, and they sat upon them, and judgment was given unto them: and I saw the souls of them that were beheaded for the witness of Jesus, and for the word of God, and which had not worshipped the beast, neither his image, neither had received his mark upon their foreheads, or in their hands; and they lived and reigned with Christ a thousand years.

All these Christians were accounted worthy of being in the first resurrection.

To be clear, over thousands of years, all those who died after living a godless and immoral life will miss out on the opportunity to live and reign with Christ in the Kingdom of God all through the Millennium. Those who choose now in this era not to give up their own reprobate life will have to wait dead in the grave until the second resurrection to life.

Revelation 20:5 But the rest of the dead lived not again until the thousand years were finished.

However, those Christians who have lived a life of responding to God's Spirit, and those who are alive at His second coming will be rewarded for their works by rising to meet Christ in the air when he comes.

Revelation 20:5b This is the first resurrection. 6 Blessed and holy is he that hath part in the first resurrection: on such the second death hath no power, but they shall be priests of God and of Christ, and shall reign with him a thousand years.

Where Does the New Covenant Fit In?
To those who understand "the Mystery", The New Covenant no longer is an agreement that they are part of. The reason for this is simple. Since 63 AD, those of us who have accepted the legal position of "the Mystery" are now reckoned by the Father as a "NEW RACE" who are neither Jews nor

Gentiles. We are now members of the very household of God and reigning, in a legal sense, with Christ Jesus at the right hand of the Father.

The New Covenant agreement, however (along with the Old Covenant), was made solely with the human nations of Israel and Judah

Jeremiah 31:31 Behold, the days come, saith the LORD, that I will make a new covenant with the house of Israel, and with the house of Judah:

This is speaking of a future time as well as in the time Christ through Jeremiah was talking about.

Hebrews 8:8 For finding fault with them, he saith, Behold, the days come, saith the Lord, when I will make a new covenant with the house of Israel and with the house of Judah:

This is when once again in the future Israel will have a new relationship with God.

Hebrews 10:16 This is the covenant that I will make with them after those days, saith the Lord, I will put my laws into their hearts, and in their minds will I write them;

The New Covenant will be re-instituted by Christ with Israel and Judah during the Millennium, but they are certainly not aware of it now.

Gentiles were never included in the agreement. For the first thirty years of Christian teaching, all the inheritance that the apostles knew about was that associated with the New Covenant made with Israel and Judah.

This is why Christ through Paul considered it necessary to find a method by which the Gentiles could become spiritual Israelites

Romans 11:23 And they also, if they abide not still in un-belief, shall be grafted in: for God is able to graft them in again. 24 For if thou wert cut out of the olive tree which is wild by nature, and wert grafted contrary to nature into a good olive tree: how much more shall these, which be the natural branches, be grafted into their own olive tree? 25 For I would not, brethren, that ye should be ig-norant of this mystery, lest ye should be wise in your own conceits; that blindness in part is happened to Israel, until the fulness of the Gentiles be come in. 26 And so all Israel shall be saved: as it is written, There shall come out of Sion the Deliverer, and shall turn away ungodli-ness from Jacob:

God showed Paul a way that Gentiles became "Israelites." They were spiritually 'grafted' into Israel without being circumcised. Indeed, all that was required of Gentiles is that they repent, accept Christ, be baptized, take the Lord's Supper and keep the minimal laws made by the apostles at Jerusalem

Acts 15:28 For it seemed good to the Holy Ghost, and to us, to lay upon you no greater burden than these neces-sary things; 29 That ye abstain from meats offered to idols, and from blood, and from things strangled, and from fornication: from which if ye keep yourselves, ye shall do well. Fare ye well.

And while the New Covenant legislation is still in effect for those who wish to join Israel and inherit only the promises given to Abraham, Isaac and Jacob (and added to by David), those of us who are part of "The Mystery" have a more majestic inheritance.

God has a much greater reward in mind for the human race than the New Covenant promises to Israel and Judah.

With the advanced teaching of "The Mystery," a Christian is no longer reckoned by God as an Israelite (or even as a Gentile either). And while the earlier promise of the New Covenant was that Israel would inherit a physical kingdom of God that will last for a Millennium is still quite valid, we have been given something more glorious.

Philippians 3:20 For our ~~conversation~~ *citizenship (Greek* poli>teuma) *is in* **heaven***; from whence also we look for the Saviour, the Lord Jesus Christ:*

Strong's 4175 *poli>teuma, — pol-it'-yoo-mah; from (4176) (politeu>omai); a community, i.e. (abstract) citizenship (figurative).*

Certainly God will keep His agreement with Israel, but we have been granted something far beyond the Kingdom. We now are a part of the very Family of God. We are no longer a part of human "Israel." As Christians, we are now a part of the divine God.

1 John 3:2 Behold, what manner of love the Father hath bestowed upon us, that we should be called the sons of God: therefore the world knoweth us not, because it knew him not. 2 Beloved, **now** *are we the sons of God, and it doth not yet appear what we shall be: but we know that, when he shall appear, we shall be like him; for we shall see him as he is.*

Since we have "died" to being human "Israelites," the New Covenant has no relevance to us any longer. We have advanced beyond it.

The Lord's Supper (which is associated with the New Covenant) no longer pertains to us. Indeed, the Lord's Supper was to show in symbol the death of Christ "until He comes back to earth." But we are now reckoned as "resurrected" with Christ and we are already legally and spiritually living

in Him in heaven. We are sitting with Him on His glorious throne next to the Father!

Ephesians 2:5 And hath raised us up together, and made us sit together in heavenly places in Christ Jesus: We are now in the ultimate state of glory.

All those who are 'the called' can boldly grasp our inheritance, our 'lot', that we are now based "IN CHRIST". Amen!

Postscript: Thanks be to our Lord Christ Jesus who inspired Ernest L. Martin to make the 'Mystery' so wonderfully clear, and for the opportunity to include extracts of his work in this final chapter.

Lightning Source UK Ltd.
Milton Keynes UK
UKOW01f1025301017
311872UK00005B/152/P

9 780994 339133